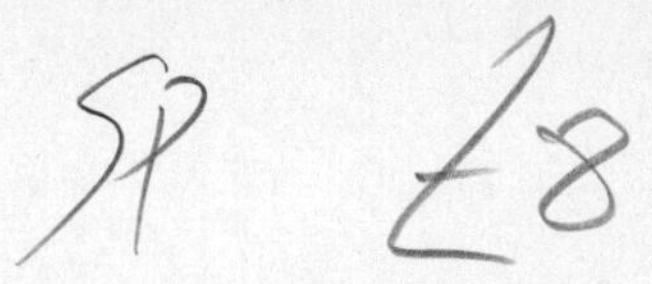

GW01607000

Economic Theory and Ideology

Economists are often struck with naive astonishment 'when what they have just thought to have defined with great difficulty as a thing suddenly appears as a social relation and then reappears to tease them again as a thing, before they have barely managed to define it as a social relation,' I.I. Rubin, *Essays on Marx's Theory of Value*, Black and Red, Detroit, 1972, p. 29, quoting from Marx's *A Contribution to the Critique of Political Economy*, Charles M. Kerr and Co., Chicago, 1904, p. 31.

Economic Theory and Ideology

Ben Fine

Edward Arnold

First published 1980 by
Edward Arnold (Publishers) Ltd
41 Bedford Square, London WC1B 3DQ

Fine, Ben
Economic theory and ideology.
1. Economics
I. Title
330.1 HB87

ISBN 0-7131-6267-8
ISBN 0-7131-6268-6 Pbk

Printed and bound in Great Britain by
Spottiswoode Ballantyne Ltd., Colchester and London

Contents

Introduction

This book is intended to present clear expositions of certain areas of economic theory with the ultimate purpose of exposing the theory to a thorough critique. The result has been that it is the essential elements of the theories that have been discussed rather than the elaborate details. There have also been excursions into the history of economic thought. In these instances, the various economists have at times been dealt a rough justice by way of representation. But then this book is concerned with a critique of economic theory rather than with its history, so that economists have been taken as representatives of certain modes of thought rather than as subjects for intellectual biography.

Each essay is intended to be self-contained, but each sheds light on the others. This makes the ordering of the chapters difficult to decide. The first chapter is concerned with economic ideology, theory and methodology in general. It could as well be read last. The second chapter analyses the aggregate circulation of capital and consequently considers capitalism's economic structure of production, distribution and exchange, an important element within which the other chapters are located. The next two chapters examine Keynesian theory and inflation theory, and each provides elements that are absent from and complementary to the other. This is followed by two chapters which deal with the school of economic theory that has been inspired by Sraffa. Where his followers would claim a critique of neo-classical economics and reconstruction of Marxist economics, we have tried to show respectively that a reconstruction of neo-classical economics and departure from Marxism is the result. The final chapter constructs an overview of the history of economic thought.

In this book, there is no systematic presentation of an alternative body of economic thought. It was, however, written from a perspective based on Marxist economics, and the author's views within this controversial subject can be found by reference to the items given in the preliminary reading. This gap in the book is partly dictated by considerations of space, but more significantly by the objectives of the book. Apart from exposing the limitations of orthodox economic theory, it is hoped that this will stimulate an interest in the alternative body of knowledge that is inspired by Marx's political economy.

Ben Fine February, 1979

Preparatory Reading

A certain knowledge of Marxist and bourgeois economics is an essential prerequisite for an understanding of this book. For an elementary introduction to the former, see B. Fine, *Marx's Capital*, Macmillan, 1975, and for a more advanced treatment, B. Fine and L. Harris, *Rereading 'Capital'*, Macmillan, 1979. There is, however, no substitute for reading *Capital*. A critical review of bourgeois economics may be found in the two books edited by F. Green and P. Nore, *Economics: An Anti-Text*, Macmillan, 1977 and *Issues in Political Economy*, Macmillan, 1979.

1

Economic Theory and Ideology

i. What is Ideology?

It is usual to view an ideology as a set of beliefs about society. These beliefs may be more or less general but they provide a framework within which the individual understands and participates in society. Of course, participation in society and thinking about it can lead to a change or development in the ideology adopted by the individual. In these terms, the study of the formation of ideologies would be reduced to a study of the influences on individual thinking. Of paramount importance would be the ideas propagated by educational institutions and the media. In general, the ideology generated is considered to consist of beliefs of two types, those that are true and those that are false. The more the influences on ideology are those that produce true beliefs the better is the state of society, although on the contrary it has been argued that a little knowledge can be a dangerous thing. Because all ideology is considered to contain some false doctrines, to label something as ideological is to use a pejorative term, to label the system of thought as non-scientific. At its worst, an ideology is reduced for its survival to the expedient of utilizing propaganda as the means of gaining influence.

The above view of ideology has certain strengths. Ideologies are not coherent systems of thought, free of inconsistencies. This is a product of their being appropriated by individuals from a multitude of sources and influences. It is also observed that ideologies contain elements of truth and elements of falsehood, and this is related but not identical to the inconsistencies of ideologies. However, the above account also has certain weaknesses. First, it presumes that there is a clear demarcation between what is true and what is false, ideology containing more or less of one at the expense of another. But even at the level of theoretical discourse, where the inconsistencies of ideology are presumed to have been eliminated, there are no agreed criteria for determining what is true and, even where there are, disagreement can still remain.

Second, the previous account of ideology is presented simply in terms of the mechanisms acting on an individual coupled with the individual's thought responses to these influences. In other words, it only deals with marginal changes in ideological developments, although these may be large. A prior question has been begged, that concerning the formation of the individual's ideology before changes are wrought in it by his own thinking and the influences on it. This question can be avoided by treating it as representing the personal history of the individual concerned. Born with a blank mind, or one merely containing a number of natural and common instincts, together with a number of individual abilities, the individual builds up an ideology of accumulated knowledge according to his life's experiences. The problem with this account is that it would lead us to believe that there are as many ideologies as there are individuals. It would deny the existence of ideologies as social phenomenan except in so far as a group of individuals more or less accidentally share a series of beliefs and an interest in propagating them. In contrast, in the remainder of this section, we shall be concerned with the question of how ideological *social* relations exist as a precondition for the formation of individual consciousness. We shall not deal directly in this chapter or even elsewhere in the book with the earlier point raised concerning the criteria for the validity of knowledge. Nevertheless, some light will perhaps be shed indirectly on this question by the discussion of other related issues.

The idea that ideologies exist as a result of the interaction of individuals with given sets of beliefs that are consequently transformed, the whole process to be repeated, is itself ideological. Interestingly, it is directly analogous to neo-classical economic theory. There, individuals come to the market, rather than the debating forum, with their factor endowments, rather than their beliefs. The exchange of goods corresponds to the exchange of ideas, and each individual goes away with something different from what he brought, these differences being determined by the aggregate and simultaneous interaction of the supply and demand for goods on the one hand and ideas on the other. Of course, just as collusion and the formation of monopolies can obstruct the harmonious and optimal exchange of goods, so can the monopolization of the media and schools and the use of false reasoning upset the free interchange of ideas. The path to truth would be hindered by the formation of an ideology.

To the individualism of neo-classical theory which leaves unexplained the social relations of capitalism, we can counterpose a theory of the economy based on the class relations associated with capital and labour. Similarly, ideological relations have to be seen as social and class relations within which individuals are located just as the individual cannot escape the economic relations associated with capital.

But what are the ideological relations associated with capital, and how are they created? The answer is to be found in the activities in which men are engaged as a result of social organization. Consider, for example, commodity fetishism. Marx argued that commodity production was a particular social form of organizing production that creates, through exchange, a definite relation between the labour of producers.

We consider this in more detail in Chapters 2 and 6, but the important point here is that this relationship between producers is expressed as a relationship between things. Two coats exchange for one chair is the way in which the connection between tailoring and carpentry is expressed and understood. Nor can anybody in capitalist society escape from this ideological understanding of commodity production except in individual thought. For just as an individual purchaser cannot in general transform the relationship that he has with the producer, so he must engage with the seller in the reified relations of exchange dictated by commodity production. Individuals are forced to conduct exchange relations as if they were relations between things, by handing one thing over for another.

It follows from the above example that ideology does not necessarily depend upon the use of false reasoning nor on falsehoods. It is in fact true that individuals engage in relations in which commodities are treated as things rather than as the products of labourers organized in definite social relations. As a result, ideology in this case can be seen to be based upon a partial and incomplete view of society in which the immediate phenomena associated with individual experience come to the fore. In other words, ideology is concerned with real appearances, although as we have observed earlier the individual understanding generated may be incoherent as these appearances are drawn from many experiences and not necessarily systematically and consistently reordered.

To generalize our understanding of ideology from commodity fetishism can, however, be misleading. For commodity fetishism is an ideological product of capitalism that blesses both capitalist and labourer although it serves the interests of capitalists by desocializing individual understanding of capitalist society. More generally, ideological relations are not symmetrical in this way, rather they reflect the material domination exercised over labour by capital in the social organization of the two classes. Consider, for example, the organization of the production process whether directly in the factory or indirectly through the search for markets and finance. It is a necessary characteristic of the existence of capital that immediate control of these processes is appropriated from the labourer and resides in the hands of the capitalist or his managerial agents. Consequently the ideological relation is created whereby the labourer is denied knowledge of the organization of production, whether this concerns technical knowledge or other managerial skills. It is not simply a case of the worker being forbidden knowledge of what goes on around him or of his having no personal financial interest in anything other than his own job. Rather, he is necessarily denied practical access to the control of production and instead is controlled in production. The material domination of the worker in the production process is the source of an ideological relation concerning access to knowledge of the production process and the instruments of control. Of course, the worker also has a knowledge that is denied to the capitalist, namely, the organization of resistance to capitalist control. Nevertheless, it is the domination by the capitalist that must prevail in general even where workers gain access to information concerning the factory through some form of workers' participation. For then, either this represents a means of moderating workers' resistance through the absorption of their leaders into management, or the workers' control becomes governed by the less direct mechanism of exchange relations that coerces the pursuit of profitability individually through the need for productivity increase. The control of production is therefore not just based upon individual relations within the factory but is a function of the capitalist relations of production as a whole. Whether considered individually or socially, the result is the same. The material relations into which workers enter tend to support the ideology that they are unable to control production. They are considered unable to control production because of their lack of managerial skill. Indeed, the neo-classical theory of resource allocation would argue that those with managerial skills or potential will be assigned through the market to their appropriate place and rewarded for their scarce abilities accordingly. Alternatively, it can be argued that workers lack the profit motive and therefore are not motivationally suitable to exercise control. These arguments have the validity of real appearances since workers are denied access to the knowledge and the motivation to organize capitalist production. However, because they do not explain the relations by which that access is denied, the argument cannot be generalized to assert that workers are unable to organize production at all.

The preceding argument and others have shown that ideology based on real appearances is valid in the sense that it does correspond to real relations and is not simply an illusion. Commodity production is organized as a relation between things, workers are unable to control and regulate the capitalist organization of production. That these appearances are real does not render them a satisfactory analysis for they remain a partial and superficial understanding of reality. Nevertheless, the question may be raised whether the appearances on which ideology may be based can have no correspondence with reality. There is a simple answer to this question, that all appearances must have some correspondence to reality, otherwise they would not exist. For example, the mirage of an oasis exists and in this sense the mirage is a real appearance, but the mirage is not itself a direct view of an oasis and in this sense it is a false appearance. The question is whether such false appearances are also characteristic of ideology.

That the answer is in the affirmative is provided by the example of wage payments. These appear to represent a payment for the full working day of the labourer. But if this were the case then there would be no surplus value produced from which profits could be formed. Consequently, the payment of wages for the commodity labour-power creates the false appearance that the labourers' total labour time has been compensated. Here again it should be observed that this false appearance consti utes an ideological relation based on the material organization of production. There can be no escape except in individual consciousness from this appearance of capitalist society. Even the worker versed in Marxist theory will be forced to act as if paid for a full day, to accept the day's wages, just as a knowledge of optics does not make mirages go away. Perhaps another analogy will help to illustrate the point. The heliocentric theory of planetary motion has displaced the theory, indeed the medieval ideology of geocentricity. But even though this is well known, for the purposes of everyday life we lose nothing by presuming the geocentric theory. Our language of the sun rising in the east is based upon it. If, however, our lives were reorganized to involve inter-planetary travel, so the 'ideology' of a geocentric solar system would necessarily be displaced just as it has been in the physical sciences. Similarly, the false appearances generated by the wage system can only be abolished by the abolition of the wage system and not merely by one worker after another realizing that a full day's labour time is not represented by the value of wages.

Before leaving a discussion of appearances, false or real, it is necessary to make explicit a consideration that has only previously been implied in the analysis. This is that to approach ideology from the perspective of the appearances that the real world generates is not to construct a rigid distinction between the individual and the real world in which the latter projects a picture show of appearances that is viewed by the former. On the contrary, we have laid emphasis on the fact that the individual draws an understanding of the real world from the activities in which he participates, as a producer for example. This participation is necessarily an insertion into the ideological relations of society which form the basis for the development of the individual's consciousness, just as other social relations form the basis and limits on his scope of activity whether it be economic or political.

Finally, let us return to an issue raised at the beginning of this section, the connection between the existence of ideological relations and the process whereby these are concretized as ideologies through the various ideological institutions such as the educational system and the church. Here the important point is that ideological relations exist from a logical point of view prior to the institutions that specialize in perpetuating or modifying them. Nor do ideological relations become ideologies merely through these institutions. For, as we have seen, the factory for example necessarily embodies significant ideological relations as does the legal system and the market mechanism. This has the implication that ideologies are not necessarily inculcated through a conscious conspiracy to spread falsehoods by a ruling class controlling ideological institutions. Rather, because ideological relations present a number of competing and inconsistent ideologies as simultaneously possible, the supporters of any one ideology generally believe it to be true and struggle to represent the truth through gaining control of ideological institutions. Consequently, ideological struggle exists at two levels: at the level of ideological relations themselves in terms of, for example, the struggle for freedom of speech and education but also at the level of control of ideological institutions through which ideological relations materialize as ideologies. It cannot be stressed too strongly how generalized is this ideological struggle at both levels. For ideological relations are to be associated with any activity which is undertaken and consequently struggle to change the conditions of these activities necessarily involves a struggle to change the associated ideological relations. By the same token, the institutions in which these activities become concretized whether school, factory family or court-house embody an ideological control even though this may not be their predominant function.

ii. What is Theory?

The conventional view of the task of theory is that it should free itself from ideological influences, the better to be able to root out the truth. In this scheme of things, theory sets out to be a coherent, systematic and consistent body of ideas. To this end, the theorist is encouraged to stand outside society so that the neutrality and non-ideological character of his labours are guaranteed. The separation of the institutions of learning from others in society would appear to provide the ideal physical climate for the mental task of separation from society that the theorist sets himself.

But even this physical separation cannot render possible the ideal theorist. There is no escape from the ideological relations that are part of any society. More specifically, the theorist will be set problems in terms of concepts that have a social existence as a result of their being products of pre-existing ideological relations. After working on these problems, the theorist communicates the results of his labour to society, but in modes of reasoning and through channels that are predetermined. Just as the theoretical problems that reach the theorist are socially determined so whether his theoretical results gain social acceptance is more or less beyond his control. In short, it is wrong in the first instance to see theory as the product of individuals just as it is wrong to see the economy or ideology in this way. Theory must be seen as a social activity before it is seen in terms of individuals.

Nor by denying the neutrality of the theorist should we allow ourselves to accept that what distinguishes theory from ideology is that the former is coherent and systematic whilst the latter is not. Just as ideologies are drawn from definite social relations that encourage partial and disconnected views of reality, so theory is constructed on the same basis. What then distinguishes theory from ideology, if it is not the superior reasoning embodied in the one as opposed to the other?

The answer in part is not the quality of the reasoning that characterizes theory, but the object that it sets itself. Ideology results from a more or less conscious attempt by individuals to develop an understanding necessary for their insertion into the activities that they undertake. Theory is a conscious attempt to explain the relationship between the appearances that form the basis of ideologies. But theory is never simply this, for it always exists in combination with some other activity. Whether educational, political, scientific or revolutionary, the theorist is never isolated from society otherwise the theory concerned would be completely anaesthetized, it would effectively remain confined to the theorist's head or writing pad.

It follows that the theorist is not only unable to stand outside society as a theorist, as argued earlier, but is also necessarily actively engaged in society in a non-theoretical capacity, even if this activity is limited to ideological interventions as may be the case for theorists in educational institutions. In this perspective, theory, itself a product of ideological relations, is a significant factor in the formation of ideologies. As such, it has the social function of establishing a theoretical terrain in which conflicts within and between classes can be formed and resolved. Most often, the attempt to accomplish this task is made whilst denying the existence of these conflicts whether it be exemplified by the harmony of general equilibrium theory or by the supposed neutrality of technology and science.

iii. Economic Theory

We have argued in the previous section that all theory is preoccupied with the study of appearances. What characterizes a bourgeois theory is that it takes the appearances of capitalism for granted and only studies the relationship between them. It does not attempt to discover what are the relations specific to capitalism which makes these appearances peculiar to capitalism. Rather it has the function of analysing the scope for the development of bourgeois society in conceptual terms dictated by the categories of appearance. It should be observed that in these terms bourgeois theory is not necessarily an apologetic for capitalism either analytically or morally. Theories couched in the categories of appearance can predict periodic crises for capitalism or condemn the distribution of income that it produces. Nevertheless, analysis that is based on an uncritical acceptance of the clothes in which capitalism presents itself will tend to produce an ideology supporting alterations to the clothes, rather than to the mode of production itself.

For bourgeois economic theory, the appearances that form the objects of analysis are the relations of production, distribution and exchange stripped of their social significance, as categories of capitalism. Thus, production is not seen as embodying relations between classes but is characterized in terms of technical relations alone that specify the connection between a set of inputs (including labour) and a set of outputs. Exchange relations are predominantly analysed in terms of the relationship between the prices of inputs and the prices of outputs and the quantities of each good that are supplied and demanded. No attempt is made to explain why products take the form of commodities and what constitutes the social significance of production for the market. Rather, it is a question of the market acting in one way or another to coordinate with various degrees of success the interaction of aggregate supply and demand. Distributional relations are examined in terms of a special case of exchange relations in which the rate of profit acts as the price of capital and the rate of wages acts as the price of labour.

An economic theory preoccupied with appearances necessarily has a systematic tendency to analyse the economy in terms of the aggregate behaviour of individual economic agents. This follows from the real appearance of the economy as the interaction of independent individuals entering exchange relations freely and coordinated as a whole through the market mechanism. On the other hand, there are economic categories that defy the bounds that would be imposed upon them by analysis entirely drawn at the atomized level of aggregate individual behaviour. Of these the most important are the categories of wages and profits, for these represent in the form of exchange a social expression of the existence of capitalism as a class system that is difficult to dispute. Similarly, there are other categories such as prices and money that reveal the existence of capitalism as a social system more complex than the sum of its individual parts, even if in these instances the class nature of the society remains concealed.

To these problems bourgeois economic theory has two solutions. The first is to continue to deny the social quality of the capitalist economy by rejecting the existence of wages, profits and prices as categories that exist in any sense other than as a relationship between individuals. In other words, atomization is taken to its logical conclusion, each exchange represents an individual transaction so that there are no uniform levels of wages, prices and profits except in theory as an approximation to the conditions generated by factor mobility and competition and the more or less close identity between one packet of peanuts and another. Each good has to be characterized more and more finely according to the time, place, transactors and informational conditions of exchange, as the theory moves to an ever closer reproduction in thought of the real appearances of capitalist exchange. The ultimate *reductio ad absurdum* of an exact replica of real appearances is beyond the bounds of possibility so that the most atomized economic theory must still retain some elements that recognize the social character of capitalist production.

An alternative to a decline into further atomization for bourgeois economics is to rely upon an inconsistent utilization of categories that have a social significance, by employing them both as representative of social relations and as aggregated individual relations. This is most clear in analyses that treat classes as if they were individuals. For example, in theories of the economy based on class struggle over distribution, that is over the general level of wages and profits, capital and labour confront each other as aggregated groups of individuals. The struggle is representative of the net sum of a series of distributional struggles between individual workers and capitalists and a pertinent question is why these individual struggles should not be the object of analysis rather than one based on classes. Similarly, underconsumptionist theories represent the level of demand in terms of the aggregate expenditure of wages and profits. Again this merely treats class expenditure of revenue as if each class were an individual and begs the question of why these expenditures should be treated as a class aggregate rather than obtained by aggregating over the individuals in each class.

What we have shown in the previous paragraph is that economic theory, even that drawing upon a class analysis, can like ideology be inconsistent since it draws upon a competing set of appearances that are generated by capitalism. In particular, capital cannot conceal the social existence of classes since it parades them to the world in the categories, wages and profits, of political economy. Yet capital also presents the economy as a more or less coordinated aggregation of individual transactions. It is the simultaneous drawing upon these two forms in which capital appears that renders an economic theory unsystematic and inconsistent. Either the economy must be treated as an aggregate of individual behaviour — in which case society is treated as that aggregate and nothing more so that social categories are rendered meaningless — or social categories have an existence, that is independent of and must be analysed prior to individual behaviour. All economic theory that is not purely atomized must confront its relation to social categories or be rendered inconsistent.

However, we have observed in the previous section that in the conventional view theory prides itself upon the goal of consistency that it sets itself to distinguish it from ideology. How is it possible for economic theory to pursue a goal of consistency whilst remaining inconsistently caught on the horns of the dilemma posed by the dual appearances of atomization and social categories? The answer is to be found in the method utilized by bourgeois economics. In the construction of its theory, bourgeois economics adopts what we shall call the axiomatic method of deduction. On the basis of a given set of assumptions concerning, for example, consumer preferences and technical conditions of production, further propositions are logically derived, most notably by the use of mathematics. Accordingly, the economic theory generated can be considered consistent as long as the initial assumptions are not mutually inconsistent for then contradictory propositions could be deduced within the theory by deduction alone. Now from the point of view of this axiomatic logic there is no inconsistency involved in treating social phenomena such as classes as if they were individuals. It is possible to compare the appearances generated by atomization and social categories without deriving an inconsistency according to the axiomatic method of deduction. But the economic theory so constructed cannot be considered to be limited to the propositions deduced within the logic. Implicit within any such economic theory and concealed by the use of mathematical results and reasoning alone is an understanding of the structure of the capitalist economy. It is within this structure rather than in its propositions that the economic theory reproduces the inconsistencies that are contained within capitals' own representation of itself as an atomized collection of economic agents coordinated through definite social relations.

Bourgeois economics tends to avoid confrontation with the inconsistencies we have discussed because of certain other aspects of its method of analysis. First, a theory of causation is utilized which parallels the axiomatic method of deduction. From the deduction of A from B may be drawn the proposition that B causes A. For example, in the Keynesian consumption function, $C=cY$, an increase in income causes an increase in consumption. Consequently, because causation is taken to run along the lines of axiomatic deduction, the economic structure and more generally the social and historical preconditions for the existence of that structure are studiously avoided. By this approach, bourgeois economics adopts a simple unilinear concept of causation, whereas in reality there is a complex structure of causation that parallels the complex structure of social relations rather than the axiomatic method of deduction.

Second, bourgeois economics tends to utilize the method of successive approximation. Because the real world is too complex to be reproduced as a mirror image by theory, some sort of approximation has to be made to the real world in the first instance. As we have observed earlier, there is a tendency within bourgeois economics to refine its theory by moving closer to the ideal mirror image of the real world be reproducing appearances in terms of atomized economic behaviour. Such is the procedure of successive approximation as more and more 'realistic' models are built. The conflict between a method based on the motivation and behaviour of individuals and the use of social categories is only recognized in terms of the 'aggregation problem', which boils down to assuming where necessary that the aggregate variable is determined as if by a representative individual until a closer approximation is made. Whilst possibly a satisfactory linkage between individual and society in terms of the axiomatic method of deduction, the unsatisfactory result is to avoid the intrinsic inconsistency that the economics contains by dealing simultaneously with social relations and aggregate individual behaviour.

Both bourgeois economics' theory of causation and successive approximation have a close connection to the method of testing theory. A distinction is correctly drawn between the theory and the real world, but the latter is incorrectly considered to be representable through facts, observations or empirical data. Consequently, a body of neutral empirical knowledge can be utilized to test a theory in principle to see if it corresponds to the facts or not. The principles of causation embodied in the axiomatic deductions and the degree of accuracy of the successive approximation are examined in the light of their empirical explanatory power. It is not our concern here to criticize the methodology implied by this procedure, one that implies that facts can be constructed atheoretically or more generally that theories can be tested by a knowledge of the real world separate from theory. Rather, because bourgeois economics purports to test itself on the basis of external criteria, the facts, it can again avoid the test of arguments concerning the limitations of its axiomatic method of deduction, its concept of causation and its method of successive approximation. As we have seen, these are the pillars upon which the theory stands to avoid confrontation with the need to explain social categories in terms other than individual activity.

Finally, it should be noted that we have characterized in general terms some of the principle methods of analysis of bourgeois economics. We have not explained why they should have been adopted unless as a conspiratorial avoidance of a more radical methodology. Here we cannot embark upon a history of bourgeois economic methodology. Suffice it to recall that such a history would draw upon the ideological role played by economic theory as previously defined. Particular emphasis would have to be placed on the role of economics as a practical science, geared towards theorizing intervention (or non-intervention) and organization of the economy whether at the macro- or micro-level. Drawing upon the need to theorize the relation between cause and effect, in the realm of appearance with the aim of having an effect, a bourgeois economics is naturally led to a methodology based on the characteristics that we have considered. To lay emphasis on the practical imperative of economics is not, however, to ignore its role in producing ideology. The contribution to ideology of bourgeois economics, from the marginalism of the 1870s to the monetarism of the modern day might even be considered more significant than the role played by the theory in formulating policy. Nevertheless, the orientation of economics to the problem of organizing the economy remains the logically prior role.

iv. Towards a Critique of Economic Theory

On the basis of the observations that we have made on the method of bourgeois economic theory, it is possible to construct a method by which that theory can be criticized. At the outset, bourgeois economics can be read for inconsistencies. These will not be derived from within the logic of the theory itself, because we can anticipate that bourgeois ecomomics will in general eliminate these inconsistencies itself. Rather, the inconsistencies will be drawn from the questions that the theory poses which are not open to solution within the theory. These concern the relationship between social and individual categories of analysis and the explanation of the historical specificity of categories such as wages, prices and profits.

However, the internal reading of bourgeois economics for problems to which there are only solutions external to the theory cannot itself be made within a theoretical vacuum. To pose the social and historical problems that are absent from bourgeois economics is already to have some theory, however poorly developed, in which these problems can be raised. In the chapters that follow, we will be assessing bourgeois economics from a perspective rooted in Marxist political economy. For many this might suggest that the criticism of bourgeois economics is predetermined since Marxist theory is simply to be counterposed to bourgeois economics. This is not strictly true, for the theoretical terrain on which we set out is bourgeois economics. From here, inconsistencies and problems are derived the discussion and solution of which will be shown to require Marxist political economy.

By way of example, consider the problems that have arisen in the previous section with the method of bourgeois economics. Its preoccupation with appearance, its use of the axiomatic method of deduction, the method of successive approximation and a simple view of the nature of causation; all combine to confront it with an insoluble problem of reconciling the social and historical character of capitalism with the atomized behaviour of individual economic agents. Now Marxism is also concerned to explain appearances. But it departs from bourgeois economics by doing so without remaining confined to concepts of appearances alone. In other words, Marxism attempts to explain the relationship between appearances by linking these appearances to concepts drawn other than from immediate appearance. The logic of Marxism is also not confined to the axiomatic method of deduction, but depends upon a conscious exploration of the relationship between the categories of analysis as social and historical variables and not simply as economic variables. The result is that the method of successive approximation is abandoned for one that reveals the connection between abstract categories that do not belong to appearance and more complex and concrete ones that do. Simultaneously, a complex structure of causation is created in correspondence with but not identical to the analysis of the structure of relations between the categories. Consequently Marxism transforms the problem that bourgeois economics faces in dealing with the appearance of atomized economic behaviour and social categories that defy definition as an aggregate of individual activity. It does not seek to replace one model compromised by a reliance upon social and individual categories by another that forms a closer approximation by moving towards a further refinement of atomization. Rather, it asks how fundamental relations that do not belong to the immediate world of appearance, such as the class relations of production, and value, are reproduced in the form of the appearances such as wages, profits and prices, that they assume at an atomized level.

However, the criticism of bourgeois economics need not be restricted to nor be predominantly an internal reading that displaces both its analysis and mode of analysis. Earlier we have seen that ideology is composed of appearances both real and false. An economic theory can be criticized not simply by counterposing an alternative explanation of appearances but by explaining why reality appears the way it does to those theories. To return to our analogy of the competition between heliocentric and geocentric theories of the solar system, the former has the advantage of explaining why the earth should appear to be the centre around which the sun rotates. More specifically for economic theory, criticism can take the form of explaining why certain directions of causation are adopted and why successive approximation rests at one level rather than other. A full answer would require an analysis in terms of the appearances that capitalism presents of itself wedded to the particular practices in which the economic theory is engaged. In the other chapters in this book, these tasks are not fully accomplished. Whether through a lack of completed analysis or whether to aid exposition, the elements of criticism that we have presented in this section are not always made available. Hopefully those elements that are will prove a convincing refutation of bourgeois economics and a confirmation of Marxist political economy.

Further Reading

The arguments in this chapter are drawn from many sources: particularly recommended are Chapter 1 of Volume I of *Capital* for a treatment of commodity fetishism; the parts on ideology in L. Althusser and E. Balibar, *Reading 'Capital'*, New Left Books, 1970, and N. Poulantzas, *Political Power and Social Classes*, New Left Books, 1973 and *Classes in Contemporary Capitalism*, New Left Books, 1975. See also N. Geras, 'Essence and Appearance: Aspects of Fetishism in Marx's *Capital*,' in R. Blackburn, ed., *Ideology in Social Science*, Fontana, 1972; E. Laclau, *Politics and Ideology in Marxist Theory*, New Left Books, 1977, and S. Mohun, 'Economics and Ideology,' in F. Green and P. Nore, *Issues in Political Economy*, Macmillan, 1979.

2

The Structure of the Capitalist Economy

i. The Circuit of Industrial Capital

At the beginning of Volume I of *Capital*, Marx undertook what appears to be a descriptive analysis of exchange processes. He started from the presumption that there is no 'cheating' in exchange, not because this is always the case, but because if exchange is not first understood on this basis it surely cannot be understood in the more complex circumstances, in which the same commodity has different prices according to who is involved in its sale and purchase. We first consider an exchange of the type C_1-M-C_2 in which commodities C_1 are exchanged for money M which in turn is used to purchase other commodities C_2. On the assumption of equal exchange, the values of C_1, M and C_2 must be identical. Consequently the only possible motive for the exchange is for the individual concerned to substitute *different* commodities C_2 for those comprising C_1.

On the other hand, Marx defined the *general* formula of capital by the scheme M-C-M′. Here, as the exchanges both open and close with the same commodity, namely, money, the motive must be to gain more value than at the outset. The general formula of capital involves buying commodities (C with money M) in order to sell dearer (at $M' > M$). The difference between the earlier simple commodity exchange and this general formula of capital can be brought out by diagram 2.1.

The general formula for capital applies to all types of capital, whether it be merchant, interest-bearing or industrial. Moreover, this formula, as it stands, relates most specifically to merchant capital, since it excludes the process of production and appears to depend upon some sort of unequal exchange. For Marx, however, it is the movement of *industrial capital* that is fundamental, since it includes the process of capitalist production. This raises the problem of demonstrating how the general formula of capital can give rise to profits even though commodities sell at their values, without unequal exchanges.

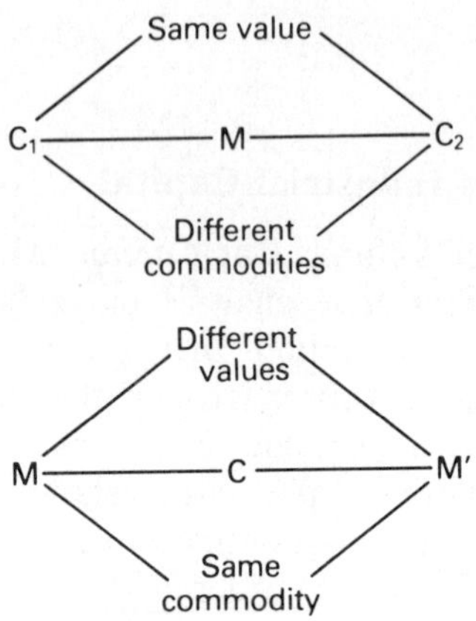

Diagram 2.1

If the exchanges M-C and C-M′ both represent value-equivalent exchanges, then for M′>M the two Cs must represent different values and consequently different bundles of commodities. The general formula of capital M-C-M′ must be broken to contain M-C as before but also C′-M′ where C′ differs from C. As a result the modified general formula is left with no process linking C and C′, M-C..?..C′-M′. It is now that we recognize that the transformation of one set of commodities C into another C′ is the function of the production process P, so that the general formula M-C-M′ becomes for industrial capital the formula M-C...P...C′-M′.

From a purely mathematical point of view, C and C′ could be the same type of commodity but of different quantities. This is, however, logically impossible, for in C must be contained the commodity labour-power LP as well as the other physical means of production MP. Whereas C′ may contain these MP, for a capitalist society it cannot include LP since labour power cannot be produced directly (although this can be done in a slave society through the production of slaves). Perhaps it should be emphasized that just as C′ neither contains labourers nor labour-power, so C does not contain labour. Although in common parlance, the capitalist is supposed to purchase labour by paying a wage, what is in fact purchased is the ability to work, labour-power. Of course, this leads to the exercise of that labour-power in the production process as labour, but neither the quality nor quantity of this labour is determined precisely in advance. This depends upon the control exerted over labour by capital in the production process.

The circuit of industrial capital that has now been constructed can best be represented as the circular flow diagram 2.2.

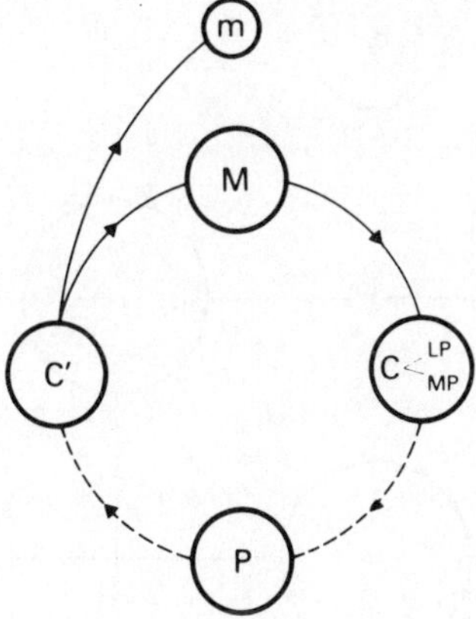

Diagram 2.2

Money M is advanced by the capitalist to purchase commodities C, composed of LP and MP. These inputs then leave the sphere of exchange and enter the sphere of production as productive capital P. After the production process P has been completed, the result is commodity capital C′ embodying a profit. This is realized as M when the commodities are sold at M′ = M + m. If the circuit is repeated, there is a continual renewal of production and exchange by which profits m are thrown off. If, however, m is capitalized and advanced as an increased money-capital, rather than being spent on consumption, then the circuit expands in spiral form.

ii. The Aggregate Circulation of Capital and Commodities

So far we have only considered an *individual* circuit of capital in isolation from its relation to other capitals. In addition, we have only examined the circuit from the perspective of its control by the capitalist. Quite clearly, in so far as the capitalist depends upon sales and purchase, some control is exerted from outside. Nor is this external control solely exerted by other capitalists as part of their circuits, for in the sale of wage-goods to workers and luxury goods to capitalists, the sales form part of a simple commodity exchange for the external agents, whose ultimate motive is final consumption. It follows that if we examine the aggregate circulation of capital, as the synchronization of many individual circuits, we must also take

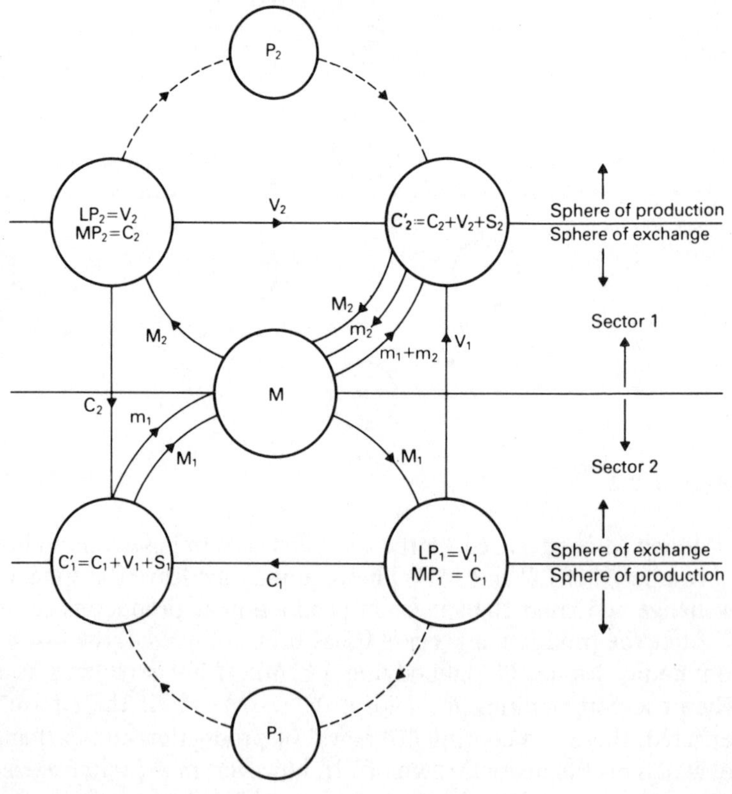

Diagram 2.3

account of many transactions that are not undertaken as part of an industrial circuit of capital. Each commodity exchange will involve at least one capitalist but not necessarily two acting as capitalists (only when one buys MP from another to renew the circuit of capital). Consequently, the aggregate circulation of capital, unlike an individual circuit, must take account of the exchange of commodities in general, from the perspective of the capitalists as capitalists as well as from the perspective of capitalists and workers as consumers.

In diagram 2.3, these points are demonstrated in the simplest possible fashion. The aggregate social capital is divided into two sectors, the first producing means of production from which only capitalists will purchase, the second producing means of consumption from which workers and capitalists as consumers alone purchase. M_i is the capital advanced as money for each sector ($i=1, 2$) $M_i = c_i + v_i$ where c_i is the expenditure on MP_i and v_i the expenditure on LP_i. After production the profit embodied in C'_i is s_i and this is realized as m_i, together with the original outlay M_i. Such an account only considers movement around each individual circuit of capital. In addition, external to each appropriate individual circuit, purchases of wage-goods $v_1 + v_2$ by workers and $s_1 + s_2 = m_1 + m_2$ by capitalists are made, as well as purchases $c_1 + c_2$ of means of production. These are indicated by arrows in the direction of purchase.

iii. Production, Distribution and Exchange

In the previous section, we have revealed the complete structure of the capitalist economy in its pure form. We have excluded casual simple commodity exchanges that are not directly related to some circuit of capital and also the intervention of other forms of capital operating to sell commodities or organize finance. We have also excluded rent. The result is to bring out the anatomy of the relationship between production, distribution and exchange for the capitalist economy, both in certain qualitative as well as quantitative respects.

In the relationship between production and exchange it can be seen in aggregate terms how the labourer and means of production are brought together for the purposes of production through exchange. For it is not simply the purchase of LP that is necessary, but also the production and sale and purchase of wage goods corresponding to that wage revenue. On the other hand, nothing more is said about reproducing labour-power, bringing workers to the market. It is presumed that the payment of wages and the production of wage-goods suffices.

In terms of the quantitative relationships between production and exchange, definite proportions must be established between the two sectors 1 and 2, if commodities are not to remain unsold or demands to remain unsatisfied. For the case of no growth simple reproduction, in which all profits are spent on consumption, we can find the condition for equilibrium from the diagram by simply equating the sales and purchases of each capital sector at C'_1 and C'_2 to obtain $c_1 + c_2 = c_1 + v_1 + s_1$ and $s_1 + s_2 + v_1 + v_2 = c_1 + v_1 + s_1$ i.e. $c_2 = v_1 + s_1$ For expanded reproduction, the sales of sector 1 must exceed the prevailing level of means of production $c_1 + v_1 + s_1 > c_1 + c_2$, and the sales of sector 2 must fall short of the total wage and profit revenue since some profits are devoted to further accumulation, $c_2 + v_2 + s_2 < s_1 + s_2 + v_1 + v_2$. In both cases this yields $s_1 + v_1 > c_2$, the extent of the inequality reflecting the extent to which resources are devoted to expansion.

In quantitative terms, the distributional relationship between capital and labour is expressed in terms of the relative sizes of $m_1 + m_2$ and $v_1 + v_2$. Clearly, it is through exchange that these quantitative relationships are brought about, but this in turn depends upon the production in the correct proportions of the commodities to which the wage and profit revenues correspond. In qualitative terms, the structural relationship between distribution and production and exchange is such that labour-power is purchased *prior* to production but profits only realized *after* production. This argument refers to the exchanges only, the actual payments may take place at a different time (in general, workers are in fact paid after some delay). Nevertheless, this is sufficient to show that it is illegitimate to consider the distributional relationship between capital and labour as simply one of division of the net product. For labour-power is paid as the precondition for the renewal of the production process, whereas profits are realized as its result. Consequently, it is not being argued that there is no struggle over the division of the net product, but that this struggle is indirect since the determination of the level of profits in response to the determination of the level of wages is mediated by the production process. In other words, it is erroneous to consider that at the end of some fictionally constructed production period, there exists a given net product to be divided between capitalists and workers. To adopt such a theoretical framework is to treat capital and labour symmetrically in distributional relations, whereas the aggregate circulation of capital reveals that their roles are far from symmetrical.

That this is so reflects the lack of symmetry of the two classes in production and exchange. Whereas each individual has a formal equality in exchange, in the sense that revenue- whether profit or wage- can purchase whatever commodities are chosen, such an equality remains a formality when the workers' expenditure is restricted to means of consumption. By the same token, the workers' sales are restricted to the commodity labour-power, since the products of labour are owned by capitalists and the worker has no other commodity to sell. A necessary element then for the existence of capital is the existence of wage-labourers who have no means of production of their own, a situation which is reproducd by the aggregate circulation of capital. This can be seen in another way. The only way in which workers can gain access to the means of production as a means of gaining work is to sell their labour-power to capitalists. For it is the characteristic of the latter class that it monopolizes the ownership and control of the means of production that comprise capital.

In the discussion so far, no reference has been made to the quantitative determination of the values c_i, v_i and s_i considered. It has been simply presumed that these are the values produced, distributed and exchanged. Now, it is well known that Marx discussed the determination of value in terms of socially necessary labour-time and it is in this sense that we shall use the term hereafter. What is less well recognized is that Marx's value theory did not simply consist of adding up the labour-time required to produce particular use values, but was based upon the fact that commodity producing societies necessarily brought different types of labour into comparison with each other through the exchange of the products of that labour. Consequently, Marx's theory concerned the form assumed by different types of labour as they were reduced to a common denominator by exchange rather than with the adding up of labour-time as such. As a result, there can be no presumption that the ratios at which commodities exchange is directly determined by the labour-time required to produce them. Nor does this, however, invalidate the location of the source of value in labour-time. For, whilst values (as measured by labour-time) may not directly correspond to exchange values, the latter do represent the fact unique to commodity-producing societies that different types of labour are being measured relative to each other through the market mechanism.

It is not our intention here to pursue these points in greater depth and detail by relating these remarks to Marx's distinction between abstract and concrete labour, the former representing through exchange the reduction of the latter to a common measure of labour-time (but see Chapter 6). In contrast, we want to turn attention away from the relationship between value and a commodity-producing society to the relationship between value and a society based on capital. For then, it can be seen that the existence of labour-power as a commodity and the ownership of the means of production by a separate class of capitalists forges a relationship of confrontation between capital and labour as classes over the production of value. This is a relationship, however, which is necessarily formed through the integration of production with distribution and exchange.

First, in production, the existence of labour-power as a commodity drives a wedge between the value of wages and the value produced by the worker during the working day. It is because it is the capacity to work that is purchased, rather than the work itself, that a difference can be created between the labour-time taken to produce the wage-bundle, and the labour-time contributed by the worker. How much this difference is depends upon the quantity and quality of work that can be extracted from labour by capital during the working day.

Second, in distribution, whilst the net value produced is $S+V = (s_1 + s_2) + (v_1 + v_2)$ which is divided into the portions of surplus value S and variable capital (paid as wages) V, these shares are not determined by profits as the residue after the deduction of wages nor vice versa. For, as we have already seen, quite apart from the level of wages paid, the surplus that emerges over and above wages is determined within the production process and depends upon the (surplus) labour that can be extracted there by capital.

Finally, in exchange, these class relations of the production and distribution of value (and surplus value) are coordinated through the formation of prices at which the exchange of values takes place.

Consequently we have no *a priori* reason to believe that commodities will exchange at ratios proportional to their respective values. Indeed, since it is the labour *embodied* in products that is exchanged, rather than the labour itself, commodities do not exchange quantitatively nor qualitatively in the form of values representing labour-time directly. As a result, prices (and wages) are formed as the means by which the values of commodities (including labour-power) are exchanged. Similarly, surplus value is simultaneously expressed by exchange in the form of profit.

Here then, we have not been concerned with the systematic influences that determine the ratios at which commodities exchange and how these depend upon the values embodied in their production. We have, however, shown how the structure of the capitalist economy brings about the formation of these exchange values in relation to the production and distribution of value. To summarize our results in another form, we have shown that capital depends upon the division of the labour of the working day into two parts V and S, the one replacing the value represented by wage goods, the other, as surplus value, forming the basis for profit. That this is possible depends upon the existence of labour-power as a commodity and the monopolization of the means of production by the capitalist class. The use of these means of production merely leads to a preservation of their value (constant capital $C = c_1 + c_2$) in the commodities for whose production they are necessary. That the production of value (and surplus value) necessarily coexists with the processes of distribution (formation of profits and wages) and exchange (formation of prices) does not negate the existence of values but locates them within the economic structure of capitalism with which they are integrated.

iv. Capital and Economic Ideology

In this section, on the basis of our previous analysis of the circuits of capital, a critique of economic ideology may be undertaken. This takes the form in part of demonstrating how capitalist relations tend to conceal themselves on the one hand, yet how they positively suggest alternative interpretations of themselves that lie within a false perspective or reveal a partial truth only.

The most obvious application of this method of criticism is the manner in which exchange relations conceal underlying class relations of production. To the individual, it is exchange relations that appear as the most immediate external, that is social, influence on economic intercourse. Consequently, just as each individual is integrated into the economy by exchanges through the market, so the economy is conceived of as the aggregation of the atomized behaviour of individuals combined and coordinated through the market. In other words, bourgeois economics becomes preoccupied with the analysis of exchange relations, most noticeably with the formation of prices through associated supply and demand schedules. The source of such a preoccupation and its correspondence with a superficial understanding of the capitalist economy is illustrated by the diagram on page 20. There it can be seen, even with a two-sector model, how the economy presents itself as the complex interaction of individual activities within the sphere of exchange. In addition, the sphere of exchange seems to divide the sphere of production into separate units and render absurd the idea that class relations of production underlie the existence of the prices, wages and profits that concern exchange activity.

Once an atomized concept of the economy has been adopted, a number of implications follow. First, it appears as if labour and physical means of production play a symmetrical role in the production of commodities. This is true of the way in which they are purchased, and it is true of their mutual interdependence in the production process. Second, then, labour, because it is symmetrically placed in relation to 'capital', is treated as a thing. It has a price, the wage, just as the price of capital is the rate of profit; it makes a contribution with capital to the production of output, and most clearly illustrative of this point, the production process is reduced to a technical relation between output and the two inputs, a conceptualization summarized in the notion of the production function. In contrast, we have already observed that the formation of wages and profits is neither a symmetrical process nor one corresponding to the formation of prices. It concerns the distributional relations between capital and labour, on the basis of exchange relations, but also on the basis of class struggle over the length and intensity of work, a factor that cannot be reduced to the technical relations of production. Just as an exchange-oriented theory leads to an atomized concept of the economy freed from the existence of classes, so is developed a concept of production freed from the existence of conflict over the production process. These elements, together with others, have the effect of denying the existence of exploitation in a capitalist society and refuting the validity of a theory of value based on labour-time. Freedom of exchange for all transactors guarantees a fair bargain between the parties concerned (given the existing distribution of resources). Quantitatively, the remuneration to capital and labour are determined by their respective contributions to output, as measured technically in neo-classical theory by marginal productivities in conjunction with the sacrifice of utility associated with abstinence and work (abstinence from leisure). In these terms, a theory of value based on labour-time is seen as an absurd denial of the symmetrical role played by capital and labour, motivated by political or ethical considerations rather than scientific reasoning.

However, we have seen that the symmetry between capital and labour is a pure formality and one that is invalidated by the consideration of capitalist social relations as a whole as opposed to an individual circuit of capital. In addition, the explanation of profits and wages (and indeed prices) on the basis of the propensity of individuals to make sacrifices of consumption and leisure and the technical relations of productions is an *ahistorical* application of the general characteristics of society to capitalism in particular. If these factors are sufficient to explain the existence of wages and profits, why have there not been wages and profits in all societies for there surely has been work and the use of physical means of production?

But to say that bourgeois economics utilizes arguments that can be characterized as ahistorical is not to categorize the theory itself as ahistorical. Quite clearly, such economic theory presupposes the existence of capitalism, the extensive development of exchange relations incorporating labour as well as its products. This is most clearly expressed in the theory's use of categories such as profits and wages, which are not only transparently specific to capitalism, but which have an intimate connection to its class relations, being the respective forms of revenue received by capital and labour. For an atomized theory, how can categories reflecting the class basis of society be incorporated?

For neo-classical theory, there are essentially two answers. The first is to deny the general categories of wages and profits, and to argue that each capitalist and worker receives a reward corresponding to the individual characteristics of the sacrifices made and their contribution to production. Here we have atomization taken to its logical limits. For analytical purposes, the differences between individuals predominate over any shared characteristic (such as class membership). Secondly, neo-classical theory can reorganize the capitalist categories of wages and profits by aggregating over classes to give rise to a representative capitalist and a representative worker (as, for example, in the aggregate production function). Such a situation has the property of treating the relations between classes as a relation between (two) individuals, a theoretical approach often employed by the cruder forms of Marxism, but one that has already been shown to be erroneous since the aggregate circulation of capital cannot be reduced to the aggregate circulation of its individual parts. Nor should it be presumed that it is only neo-classical economics that, confining itself to an analysis of exchange relations, confronts the existence of categories associated with capital's class relations by the treatment of those relations as if they were ones between individuals.

Consider, for example, those theories usually described as neo-Ricardian or Sraffian, that analyse the capitalist economy in terms of a distributional struggle between capital and labour over a net product that is determined on the basis of given technical conditions of production. The net product of the theory is to recognize the existence of the class relations specific to capitalism by reference to a derived inverse relationship between wages and profits. But, in strict analogy with the neo-classical theory of the marginal productivities of *aggregate* factor inputs, it does so in a way that treats capital and labour as if they were two individuals. The bully struggles for a share of his victim's iced bun!

Alternatively, capital and labour can be treated, through the expenditure of wages and profits, as the two individual sources of effective demand. This is so in the Keynesian theories associated with Kaldor and Kalecki, or in Marxist terminology, the underconsumptionist theories most recently associated with Baran and Sweezy. In contrast to the orthodox Keynesian categories of effective demand, such as consumption, investment and other autonomous expenditure, these theories utilize the categories of wages and profits which immediately reflect the existence of capital's class relations. On the other hand, they do so in a way that remains confined to the sphere of exchange. Consequently, once again, the classes are treated as individuals (as buyers and sellers), just as earlier we saw them treated as individual antogonists in the distribution process and factors of production in neo-Ricardian and neo-classical theory respectively. Finally, the exchange-based treatments of classes can be combined, so that capitalism becomes understood as a system based on the interaction of a distributional struggle between capital and labour and the aggregate demand generated by the resulting levels of wages and profits. Such a theoretical framework is made explicit by Nell (1972) who correctly argues that it underlies the work that constitutes radical political economy and its revival.

Our earlier analysis of the aggregate circulation of capital and commodities demonstrate not only how profits and wages are produced, distributed and exchanged, but also how these elements of the economy are reproduced. What is involved is a continuous motion and unity of the circuits of capital. However, a partial understanding of reproduction will be obtained by focusing upon one particular form of capital in the aggregate circulation and examining its point of departure and arrival.

For example, if we consider an individual circuit of capital, abbreviated to the form M....M′, then it is the use of money in the process of exchange that appears to explain the expansion of exchange value (and creation of profits) and so the return of the initial advance also. The initial advance of money as capital can be set against the alternative choice of expenditure on consumption, so that abstinence becomes an explanatory element of reproduction. Because the process of reproduction is reduced to a one-dimensional denominator in the form of money, profit becomes confused with the rate of interest (as in Fisherian theory) and is explained in terms of the natural productivity of time (most notably in the early Austrian marginalists' concept of the productivity of roundabout methods of production, or the analogies drawn between the growth of capital and the growth of trees).

Alternatively, if we examine reproduction in the abbreviated form P...P, the relationship between inputs and outputs forms the focus of attention. In contrast to reproduction considered in the form of M....M′, where the process of production interrupts the process of money-making through exchange, it is here that exchange appears as an unfortunate obstacle in the expansion of production. Where possible, the necessity of buying and selling (at a profit) is ignored, a theoretical approach that leads to the adoption of Say's Law as a means to concentrate on the technical relations of production and the distribution and price relations with which they are integrated.

Such a perspective characterizes the school of classical political economy as well as modern neo-classical growth theory and the linear models associated with von Neumann and Leontief.

Finally, economic reproduction can be considered in the form C′....C′. On this basis, production and consumption are united in the commodity as it emerges from the production process to find its place on the market. Within neo-classical general equilibrium theory and those theories that reduce Adam Smith's invisible hand to an ideology of the efficiency of laissez-faire economy, the unity of production and exchange accomplishes an harmonious and optimal equilibrium, for which the ultimate criterion of economic activity is consumption (and not profit). This is not, however, a necessary conclusion as witnessed by Keynesianism, which theorizes an equilibrium at less than full employment. Another question that may be posed within this approach is the quantitative division of the surplus as it emerges, embodied in commodities and to be realized as profits etc., as well as to be divided between final consumption and investment. But, as we have already observed above, to pose these questions is by no means to guarantee adequate answers.

Further Reading

This essay draws heavily upon Volume II of *Capital.* See also B. Fine, 'The Circulation of Capital, Ideology and Crisis,' Bulletin of the Conference of Socialist Economists, December, 1975. A reference in the text is made to E. Nell, 'The Revival of Political Economy,' in R. Blackburn, ed., *Ideology in Social Science*, Fontana, 1972.

3

Keynesianism: A Critique

i. Keynes and 'Classical' Theory

Keynes wrote to George Bernard Shaw about his General Theory that 'To understand *my* state of mind, however, you have to know that I believe myself to be writing a book on economic theory which will largely revolutionize — not, I suppose at once but in the course of the next ten years — the way that the world thinks about economic problems.'

He went on to add that 'in particular the Ricardian foundation of Marxism will be knocked away.' By this Keynes presumably meant that the labour theory of value would give way to an alternative theory, not based on marginal productivities and marginal utilities as suggested by neo-classical economics, but one based on expectations and the rate of interest as we shall see.

Now, that Keynes should believe that he could undermine Marxism by demolishing its Ricardian foundations demonstrates that his knowledge of Marxism must have been almost as limited as Shaw's. The latter was not known for his modesty in matters of intellectual capacity. Of his own *Collected Plays* (comprising a volume of 1200 closely printed pages), he judged a full understanding could only be obtained on the basis of a reading once every six months for a period of ten years. By contrast, he claimed to have read and absorbed the works of Marx in a single afternoon! Nor can we acknowledge Keynes a modest man, but history seems to have absolved his claim to fame as a revolutionary leader in economic theory. 'We are all Keynesians now' runs the well known cliche (but as 1984 approaches Orwellian monetarists would presumably point out that some are more so than others). It is our task to examine the content of Keynes's contribution, locate it within the tradition of Keynesianism that it inspired and finally discover the relation of Keynesianism to that theory which in Keynes's words lives 'below the surface, in the underworld of Karl Marx'.

To understand why Keynes considered his contribution to be a revolutionary impetus to economic theory, it is necessary to understand the contributions of pre-Keynesian economic theory to the field of what was to become macro-economics. Keynes entitled his magnum opus 'The General Theory of Employment, Interest and Money.' He might just as well have entitled it 'The General Theory of Unemployment, Interest and Money.' For it is Keynes's concepts of unemployment, the rate of interest and money that were so radically different from those of his predecessors. This led Keynes to dismiss together the classical and marginal economists as being unable to deal with the concept of effective demand. He viewed Ricardians and marginalists as brothers in economic theory, all to be classified as 'classical' for their adherence to Say's Law, despite the fact that the two schools did differ over their understanding of the causes of unemployment (the Ricardians emphasizing Malthusianism and diminishing returns to scale and deviations around a stationary state, the marginalists considering deviations around what would now be considered general competitive equilibrium).

Before considering Keynes's critique of Say's Law, let us examine the pre-Keynesian theories of interest and money. At its best, 'classical' theory simply identified the rate of interest with the cost of borrowing, so that it would form a portion of the economic surplus, to be appropriated by lenders in return for their abstinence. As such, the rate of interest could be distinguished from the rate of profit. At its worst, however, 'classical' theory simply identified the rate of interest with the rate of profit, most notably in the Fisherian theory. There, the rate of interest/profit is determined by intertemporal preference between present and future consumption together with intertemporal production possibilities.

The 'classical' theory of money was extremely underdeveloped, but not in the sense that the functions of money were not recognized. That money is a means of payment, unit of account and store of value was as well recognized in the nineteenth century as it is now. However, as is easily seen, money plays no role in the construction of the stationary state, in theorizing general equilibrium and in analysing the deviations from these organizing concepts of 'classical' theory. Money simply acts as the neutral medium through which exchange takes place. Like the air we breathe, it was as necessary in reality as it was unnecessary in theory. As a result, pre-Keynesian monetary theory is dominated in one form or another by the quantity theory.

The underdevelopment of the role played by money in 'classical' theory is reflected in the adoption of Say's Law of markets. It is based on the principle that whenever an individual plans a demand for some commodities of some value, a simultaneous plan must be made to make a supply of other commodities of equivalent value. Consequently for each individual, notional or planned demand must equal notional supply. Otherwise individuals would be irrationally anticipating supplying more value in commodities than they receive in return or expecting some other individuals to act in this fashion so that more value in commodities is demanded than is supplied. What is at issue here is not some unequal value exchange between individuals. Whatever prices individuals confront each other with (and they can differ between transactions if so desired), each individual must plan to make sales (value of supplies) to match the planned purchases (value of demands). Moreover, what is true for each individual in this case must also be true for the economy as a whole. The aggregate planned demand for commodities must precisely match the aggregate planned supply (although, of course, the aggregate planned demand for each commodity may not match the planned supply; this would depend upon relative prices and hence the need for a fictional Walrasian auctioneer to adjust prices and grope to equilibrium).

It is important to emphasize that we have only been dealing with commodity markets so that money is not only a veil but also excluded. We return to this below as a point of departure for Keynesian from pre-Keynesian economics. In addition, we have only been considering notional supply and demand. Now, to obtain Say's Law, we make the heroic assumption that each notional supply and demand is not simply confined to the individual's head but makes its presence felt on the market concerned. Consequently, if a supply meets a demand and vice-versa, all is well and good. Otherwise an excess supply or an excess demand will be created respectively. In short, Say's Law involves making the leap from the existence of notional to the existence of *effective* demands and supplies.

Once we make this leap, the equality of aggregate notional supply and demand becomes transformed into the equality of aggregate effective supply and effective demand. Put another way, corresponding to the excess demands in some markets, there must exist corresponding excess supplies in other markets. Demand creates its own supply and supply creates its own demand (but not necessarily in the correct markets unless equilibrium is achieved).

An immediate implication of Say's Law, and one that is crucial for understanding 'classical' theories of unemployment, is that there cannot be general over-production, excess supply of all commodities, for then aggregate supply could exceed aggregate demand. It follows that disequilibrium takes the form of excess supply in some markets and excess demand in others. In addition, it is natural to presume that such disproportions will be self-righting since prices will rise (fall) in markets characterized by excess demand (supply), tending to correct the imbalance within the market by an increase (decrease) in supply and decrease (increase) in demand.

For classical political economy proper, the predominant explanation of unemployment was to be found in the excess supply of labour that could be temporarily generated by the Malthusian law of population. An excess demand for labour corresponds to an excess supply of (corn-) capital, wages being forced above subsistence and inducing population growth. On the other hand, an excess supply of labour corresponds to an excess demand for capital (corn-wages), wages being forced below subsistence thereby decreasing unemployment through destruction of the labour-force. Unemployment occurs when the economy grows beyond the stationary state.

To emphasize the fluctuations on the labour market as a whole for classical theory is not to suggest that the theory is unaware of the possibility of over-production in some sectors, but under-production in others, creating excess supply and demand respectively for the labour in those markets. But then, market forces of competition are seen as the agency for making this disequilibrium temporary, excess supply and demand being eliminated by the appropriate price and quantity movements. It should be observed, however, that the process of restoring equilibrium in labour markets is exactly the same whether considered in aggregate or sectorally, but that the agent restoring equilibrium is the Malthusian Law of population in the one case, but market competition in the other. The production of labourers is treated in effect like the production of any other commodity, as responding to the wage its market price.

The marginalist revolution of the 1870s, that has dominated economic theory up to the time of the Keynesian revolution (and beyond), contained its own 'stationary state', namely general equilibrium. Attention is increasingly focused on the static properties of this equilibrium, as economics replaces political economy and becomes the theory of efficiency and optimality. The classical theory of value, class and distribution gave way to a methodology of atomization, maximization, and distribution as price theory, all harmonized by the freely enjoined market mechanism. Whilst the differences between this methodology and that of the classicals cannot be over-emphasized, for Keynes the two were to be identified for their reliance upon Say's Law. True, this had the implication that both theories equated aggregate supply and demand. In addition, competitive forces reduce individual excess demands and supplies to zero by the appropriate price and quantity movements. Thus, on the face of it, one would have expected the neo-classical and classical theories of crisis to be identical, as suggested by Keynes's all-embracing 'classical'.

Nothing could be further from the truth, as is exemplified by the respective theories of the forces operating in the labour market. For classical theory, this revolved around the Malthusian theory of population. Unemployment of resources is only possible when the stationary state has been over-reached, and it is labour that would be unemployed, because there would not even be subsistence wages available to go round. But, in neo-classical theory, the labour market, like everything else, depends upon the productivity and utility (in this case disutility) of labour. Given the marginalist stress on the substitutability between factors, this would leave no room for unemployment at all, provided that every factor is prepared to receive its marginal product as its price. Here is the proviso for neo-classical theory that explains unemployment. It is not due to over-population, but to over-pricing. If labour, like any other factor, is unemployed, this must reflect that its price, wages, are too high and that the mechanism for eliminating unemployment should be market forces. The logic of the neo-classical theory leads to a justification for wage cuts and the removal of any impediments, such as trade union activity, to the achievement of them through the free play of market forces. Here, at least, is one strand of neo-classical ideology that can survive the Keynesian revolution!

ii. Effective Demand, the Multiplier and Involuntary Unemployment

For our purposes, however, the differences between neo-classical and classical theories are at best an interesting digression because for Keynes emphasis needed to be laid upon their common reliance upon Say's Law. A central feature of Keynes's thought is to reject Say's Law and to take a different view of the way in which the market worked. For him, the 'classical' theory was based upon a system of aggregate supplies and demands built up according to prevailing prices. A corresponding system of excess supplies and demands is created, stimulating price changes and so the whole process repeats itself in its movement toward equilibrium. The implied harmonious interaction of supply and demand has been called a 'quantity responding to price' system, for this is the basis on which individuals or sectors of the economy treated as individuals are seen to behave, even if in aggregate prices do in turn respond to quantities.

In contrast, Keynes would have admitted the possibility of a 'quantity responding to quantity' system. What does this mean? Well, the basis of Say's Law is that every supply is a demand, not only for actual quantities exchanged but also for notional supplies and demands. But what this law confuses is that whilst in any actual transaction, the supply and demand are necessarily realized simultaneously, for any individual transactor the balancing acts of supply and demand are separated in time and space. By the same token, notional supplies and demands can only effectively be felt upon the market, when each and every one is completely and correctly sequenced.

For example, consider an economy consisting of three individuals (or sectors), investment goods, consumption goods and labour. The first sector, we shall presume, uses C_1 investment goods annually, employs labour of value V_1 and makes profits S_1. The second sector has corresponding quantities C_2, V_2 and S_2. Labour services of value V_1 plus V_2 are supplied to the economy as a whole. We shall assume that all profits are spent on consumption goods. As a result, it is quite simple to draw up a picture of sales and purchases with the arrows denoting purchase, as in diagram 3.1.

Sector 1 buys V_1 from workers and S_1 from sector 2, which in turn buys C_2 from sector 1 and V_2 from workers, who buy V_1 and V_2 from sector 2 having sold total labour services of that value.

Now suppose that a worker became unemployed, say in sector 1: Then he is unable to purchase wage goods from sector 2, which in turn is unable to purchase investment goods from sector 1, having found deficient demand for its consumption goods. Sector 1 then finds deficient demand for its goods and so is persuaded that the unemployed worker should remain so. (In addition, if the unemployment leads to a loss of profits further deficient demands may result.)

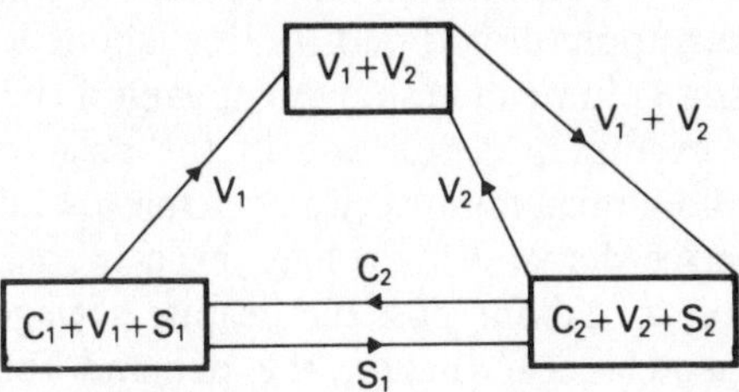

Diagram 3.1

The economy is caught in a vicious circle. Say's Law holds *in principle. Notionally*, there is an excess supply of labour matching an excess demand for goods. But there is no reason why these notional supplies and demands should be felt on the market. Nor is the problem to be based necessarily on the existence of non-equilibrium prices. Indeed, all exchanges could be taking place at equilibrium prices! There is no reason for this unemployment disequilibrium to be broken, since it is not because prices are wrong that each transactor is unable to sell the appropriate goods but because each depends on the others' transactions. By way of analogy, consider individuals crowded together on a race-track. Each can only go around as fast as the one in front. But the one in front of each individual runner is ultimately the individual himself. Now, in the economy, we can see (by considering the sales and purchases of either sector 1 or sector 2) that an equilibrium 'pace' of production is given only when $C_2 = V_1 + S_1$ or $C_2 + V_2 = S_1 + V_1 + V_2$ respectively. But it is quite possible that the pace of production that prevails is not the one to be associated with full employment.

Many of you will already have associated this description of the market mechanism with the Keynesian multiplier. For this, it is precisely changes in the level of investment (or other autonomous expenditure) that generate an extra income according to the additional effective demands that flow through the system, creating employment and output, their depending quantitatively on the marginal propensity to consume. Conversely, corresponding to ineffective demand, Keynes constructed the notion of involuntary unemployment. We have already seen that involuntary unemployment can arise irrespective of the level of real wages, in particular even if the marginal product of labour equals the real wage.

Keynes defined involuntary unemployment, the possibility of which he argued 'classical' theory could not allow, as a situation in which both the supply of and demand for labour would be greater than the existing volume of employment even if the real wage were reduced. (For example, an increase in the price of wage goods). How this should come about need not detain us here. Suffice it to note that effective demand must have been increased to make an increased supply of labour possible despite a wage reduction. By contrast for neo-classical theory, the demand for labour would increase if the real wage fell (below the marginal product of labour) but the supply of labour would fall below the existing volume of employment, especially if in equilibrium the marginal disutility of labour were equal to the real wage and even if trade union or other collective action (strikes) held the real wage above this level. For Keynes, however, the marginal disutility of labour could be above the real wage, quite apart from the trade union 'closed shop', because of the existence of ineffective demand. He therefore rejected the 'second postulate' of 'classical' theory, that the marginal disutility of labour should equal the real wage, whilst accepting, for the sake of argument, the first postulate that the real wage equal the marginal productivity of labour.

iii. Money and Interest

This then constructs a preliminary understanding of Keynes's concept of unemployment. For neo-classical theory, the possibility of an increase in employment through an increase in the price of wage goods, impossible through a decrease in money-wages, would have to be explained in terms of money-illusion — the mistaken belief on the part of workers that their real wages had not fallen because the wage level had not fallen. However, it is important to observe that in discussing the market mechanism we have made no reference to the role played by money. The money — illusion mentioned immediately above might more accurately be characterized as real price illusion. Money has not entered the discussion so far. Our vicious circle of defective demand and unemployment could as well be occurring in a barter economy, in which exchanges are more indirect without the intervention of money but for which a sequence and synchronization of acts of exchange are still necessary. (Without money, the labourer who sells to sector 1 has to take investment goods in exchange which then are used to purchase consumption goods from sector 2, unless sector 1 capitalists have taken the initiative of exchanging their products with sector 2 in anticipation of employing labour. Clearly the equilibrium condition $C_2 = V_1 + S_1$ conceals complex interactions through the market).

A monetary economy will be more efficient in coordinating exchange, although in equilibrium the barter and monetary economies would appear to be identical. If we include money in our diagram, then indirect exchanges do not have to be made to effect the desired exchanges since money acts as an intermediary instead. Now, corresponding to every purchase there is a flow of money in the direction indicated with commodity flows in the opposite direction. It follows that if the economy is in a Keynesian unemployment equilibrium, then it is not simply quantities of commodities that do not flow but quantities of money also. These must be held in stock, like the labour of the unemployed and the idle capital and unsold commodities of the capitalists. Conversely if the money were spent, then, whether on consumption or investment, the multiplier process would be set in motion and an increase in effective demand brought about. (It is for this reason that Keynes praised Malthus's emphasis on the role played by the luxury consumption of landlords in maintaining demand and regretted the development of economic thought on the basis of Say's Law rather than principles of underconsumption.)

In this light, the formation of stocks of money becomes important. Keynes identified three motives for holding money, the transactions, precautionary and speculative demands for money. Of these, the speculative demand formed Keynes's theoretical innovation. It depends upon recognizing money as a store of value that could be immediately exchanged for commodities in the future. Money is held for speculative purposes if it is anticipated that the relevant commodities, i.e. those which are to be purchased, will fall in price. This is a readily understood phenomenon. If anybody expects the price of a commodity he means to buy to decrease, he will buy later or more exactly plan to buy later, and hold on to money. Now the concept of money as a store of value together with the 'quantity adjusting to quantity' view of the market mechanism is an important break with pre-Keynesian theory since it gives money an active role in theorizing the economy, and does not assign it the role of a neutral veil.

But for this new role of money to have any significance, two further elements are necessary — a theory of expectations and a theory of value. This is because the speculative demand for money depends upon expectations about future prices. As indicated earlier at the outset, Keynes's value theory had the intention of undermining the 'Ricardian foundations of Marxism' by undermining an objective theory based on labour-time (or more generally physical costs of production). This was not to be done by appending the subjective theory of value associated with marginalist utility theory, since this was equally open to Keynes's criticism of irrelevance to the macro-economic problem of unemployment. For it was the introduction of expectations to the central stage of economic theory that was a major innovation of Keynes. It was related to value theory through the effect of expectations on the rate of interest, and the effect of the rate of interest on the *value* of capital. As we shall see, Keynes constructed a theory of value that ingeniously depended upon the failure of the market to work rather than on an idealized account of the harmonious interaction of supply and demand. Keynes's theory of interest was essentially based on two considerations. First, the rate of interest represents the interest foregone by holding money and therefore the cost of borrowing money. Second, as such, the rate of interest represents the inverse of the price of a bond (the value of capital). A bond guarantees an annual payment of say £1 per annum (£2 per annum would form the equivalent of two bonds etc). Its value or price is its discounted present value given by $\frac{1}{1+r} + \frac{1}{(1+r)^2} + \frac{1}{(1+r)^3} + \ldots$ which is a geometric progression summing to $\frac{1}{r}$. Thus, the price of a bond varies inversely with the rate of interest. Savers buy bonds and the higher the rate of interest the better off they are, but vice-versa for borrowers.

Now there is nothing new in seeing the price of capital as the inverse of the rate of interest. It is simply present value discounting.

What is new in Keynes is the manner in which the rate of interest is determined, by the supply of and demand for capital, but in which speculation and expectations play their part as well as the Fisherian factors of intertemporal utility and production.

For simplicity, we identify the bond market with the financing of physical investment. First consider the demand for bonds, when r equals r*, the expected value of r. The demand for bonds increases with a fall in their price i.e. a rise in the rate of interest. But if r* moves above r, the price of bonds is expected to fall, the demand for bonds will also fall as savers hold money, planning to purchase bonds later. Second, however, surely capitalists who wish to make investments by borrowing would increase the supply of bonds in anticipation of a decrease in their price? (Just as savers wish to buy bonds later, borrowers wish to sell them now). The result would appear to be a shift in the supply of bonds restoring the level of investment albeit at a higher rate of interest fulfilling expectations (equilibrium at C rather than A or B). See diagram 3.2.

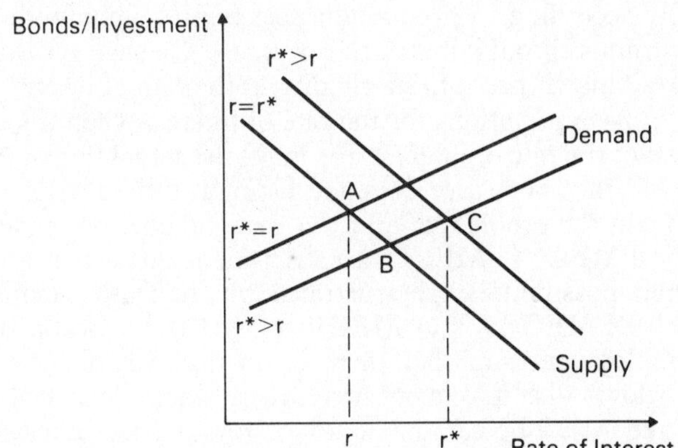

Diagram 3.2

The above argument is not entirely correct because capitalists will not invest more now because they expect the rate of interest to rise, but only invest as long as their rate of return, what Keynes called the marginal efficiency of capital (MEC), is greater than the rate of interest (although if r* > r borrowers can be expected to sell bonds quickly). As a result in equilibrium MEC = r, since investments are made until diminishing returns brings the MEC down to

r. More significantly, the MEC is not simply a physical property of the technical production possibilities over time as suggested by the Fisherian theory. Rather, it also depends upon the effective demand for products, since profitable production in accounting terms is worthless unless the products can be sold. As Marx observed, commodities are in love with money, but the course of true love never did run smooth. The same conclusion holds in the context of a Keynesian theory of effective demand, particularly when money is being held for speculative purposes in anticipation of a rise in the rate of interest. For it is the same factors that lead to an increase in liquidity preference (and increase in r^*) that may lead to pessimism about effective demand and reduce the supply of bonds.

In short, even if the MEC equals r, this could be achieved at below full employment investment because the expectation of the rising rate of interest may hold its actual value above the equilibrium level. In this case $r^* > r = \text{PMEC} = \text{MEC} > \bar{r}$ where $\bar{r}$ is the full employment equilibrium level of the rate of interest and PMEC stands for the Fisherian determination of the rate of return physically according to production possibilities alone without any sale constraints through ineffective demand. We shall return to this case below since it presumes a rigidity in the rate of interest generated by *rising* expectations for the rate of interest when the equilibrium level of the rate of interest $\bar{r}$ is *below* the actual rate of interest.

However, the above case does not distinguish the PMEC and the MEC so that the problem of effective demand does not arise! More generally, $\text{PMEC} \geq \text{MEC}$, with strict inequality when profitable production possibilities are frustrated by ineffective demand. It follows that $\text{PMEC} > \bar{r} > \text{MEC} = r < r^*$ is a logical possibility for unemployment and that there is no necessity for $\bar{r} < r$ to explain below full employment investment, since $\bar{r}$ may lie between PMEC and MEC ($\bar{r}$ cannot lie above PMEC, for otherwise full employment investment would have been reached and surpassed). This is the true example of ineffective demand. It becomes sustained as an equilibrium when r^* is restored to equality with r (but not $\bar{r}$) so that there are no further changes in expectations to stimulate changes in other variables.

iv. The Neo-Classical Synthesis

In the previous sections, we have dealt with some of the central ideas that represented innovations by Keynes and which broke with pre-Keynesian theory. The Keynesian macro-economic theory to which these ideas gave birth is the analysis based on IS/LM curves, known as the neo-classical synthesis. But it cannot be presumed that the synthesis embodies all the innovations suggested by Keynes, although it clearly includes some. The multiplier and effective demand have been the stimulus to launch macro-economics as a theoretical and empirical field of study. This is easily recognized in the study of macro-economic aggregate such as the consumption and investment functions. In addition, a great stimulus has been given to theoretical and empirical study of the demand for money, and in particular to its interest-elasticity. However, if Keynesianism has predominantly been a synthesis, of elements from Keynes and the 'classics', what are the elements that comprise the necessary compromise?

First, the multiplier and effective demand are admitted to be important for a study of macro-economics but neither the level of autonomous expenditure (and in particular investment) nor its multiplicative effects can be taken to be exogenous. They must be located in terms of a general equilibrium of the other macro-economic aggregates such as the supply and demand for money.

Second, Keynes's criticism of Say's Law is valid but only in so far as this law is restricted to aggregation over commodities alone, excluding the money market. Clearly an aggregate excess supply of *all* goods could correspond to an excess demand for money and vice-versa. Accordingly, Say's Law is replaced by Walras's Law in which all markets are included. Third, if there is an excess demand for money, there will be a corresponding excess supply of goods, investment and employment. As a result, an unemployment equilibrium will be temporarily created through the multiplier and in-effective demand.

Fourth, such a divergence from full employment equilibrium must be temporary unless there exist market rigidities restricting the movement of appropriate prices. Either prices or wages are rigid downwards so that the price level as a whole does not fall (shifting the LM). Alternatively, investment may be interest-inelastic so that when the rate of interest falls in response to declining demand for money as prices, wages and transactions fall, investment does not increase (an investment strike — the case of a vertical IS curve). Finally, the rate of interest may not fall despite declining prices, since there may be an absolute preference for liquidity (particularly if the rate of interest is expected to rise). In this case (the horizontal LM curve), the rate of interest is rigid downward and cannot move to its equilibrium level, a situation known as the liquidity trap.

Finally then, Keynes's theory is not general because it depends upon assuming (price or interest) rigidity in one market or another, precisely the circumstances recognized by 'classical' economics as a cause of disequilibrium. On the other hand, Keynes has introduced the money market into these considerations and has pinpointed the *special*, not general, case of the liquidity trap which is of considerable practical importance for reasons of realism and policy.

That the synthesis adopts some of Keynes's innovations is undeniable, the rejection of Say's Law, the importance of money, the multiplier and effective demand. But that it rejects others is equally clear. Say's Law is simply modified to Walras's Law, to include money, so that the workings of the market mechanism remain 'classical', breaking down only for price rigidities. In other words, the synthesis clings to a view of the economy predominantly as a 'quantity adjusting to price' system as opposed to a 'quantity adjusting to quantity' system. All notional demands remain effective, even if not realized, but they may meet the obstacle of market rigidities.

The synthesis' divergence from Keynes's theorizing is particularly exemplified by the argument at the end of the previous section. For the synthesis, there is no distinction between the PMEC and MEC, the individual firm is not sales (quantity) constrained, although it does face a demand curve (usually taken as horizontal). Consequently, unemployment equilibrium is necessarily characterized by $r = \text{PMEC} = \text{MEC} > \bar{r}$.

The full employment equilibrium level of the rate of interest must be below the actual rate for unemployment, the actual rate failing to fall because of some rigidity in the money market. In contrast, we have seen by drawing the distinction between the PMEC and MEC that in Keynes's system, the economy can be at unemployment equilibrium at a rate of interest below or even equal to the full employment equilibrium level. It is intrinsic to the neoclassical synthesis that one or more prices must be wrong for disequilibrium, whereas this is quite clearly not necessarily so for the economics of Keynes.

v. The Reappraisal of Keynes

In recent times, there has been a reaction against the Keynesianism of the neo-classical synthesis and the development of a reappraisal of Keynes's economics. It takes as its point of departure the significance of sales constraints on the optimizing behaviour of economic agents and consequently restores the 'quantity adjusting to quantity' element to the economic system. In particular, Clower has developed the concept of the dual-decision hypothesis. An economic agent facing a vector of prices $p_1, \ldots, p_n$ can calculate optimal sales and purchases and these form notional supplies and demands. However the ability to realize these plans depends upon them all being carried out in an appropriate sequence without, for example, a lag in plans frustrating an intended purchase. For, should this occur, then the economic agent will be forced to carry through a second optimization contingent upon the exchanges that it has proved possible to make. Hence the term dual-decision hypothesis. If we aggregate over all economic agents, we can see that their integration into a market system, in which all notional supplies and demand are not realized or even effective simultaneously, can lead to an undisturbed unemployment equilibrium in which economic agents ratify each others' constrained dual decisions. This is as true for the consumer unable to sell labour as it is for the entrepreneur unable to sell products.

It should be observed that the reappraisal does not depend upon the existence of money in the economy, for the argument above is consistent with barter-constrained optimization. But money can be added as a means of payment and speculative and liquid store of value. The reappraisal can then be seen to be a generalization of the synthesis. For, wherever the synthesis involves an optimization over price parameters alone, the reappraisal also includes quantity constraints. The one is the special case of the other in which notional supplies and demands are effective and quantity constraints not binding because prices would adjust if they were.

As such, the reappraisal would appear to be able to stake a strong claim to represent Keynes's economics since it is a generalization and not a special case of 'classical' theory and it also breaks with the 'classical' and synthesis' identification of notional and effective supplies and demands (in the form of Say's and Walras's Law respectively).

However, as it stands, the reappraisal has not theorized what constitutes the quantity constraints. What it has done is to show that their existence can lead to self-sustaining unemployment equilibrium. Clearly, the quantity constraints confront individual economic agents as social constraints, the level of demand, the cost of finance etc. The individual's reaction to these can itself be theorized in terms of the attempt to overcome them. How mobile is labour, for example, at what point do job aspirations wane as search for employment is unsuccessful, what are the forms taken by and the effects of the economic informational structure? Significantly, these are all analysable within the synthesis' framework and would have been categorized by Keynes as causes of voluntary unemployment.

It follows that within the reappraisal the quantity constraints are simply formed out of the aggregate behaviour of individuals and vice-versa as a simultaneous process coordinated through the market. In fact, as we have already observed, the reappraisal is a generalization of general equilibrium theory to take account of quantity constraints. As such, what it gains as a generalization, it loses as a theory of *macro*-economics. It becomes a theory of the economy as an aggregation of the simultaneous interaction of the optimizing (micro-economic) behaviour of individuals.

vi. The Economics of Keynes

Keynes claimed to have written a *general* theory. The advocates of the neo-classical synthesis see this as a mistaken claim, whereas for the reappraisal it is confirmed but only at the expense of sacrificing macro-economics. Now, if we are to take Keynes at his word, it follows that plenty of evidence will exist to support both of the conflicting interpretations of his work (and also explain inconsistencies within it). For, if he did indeed compose a general theory, he must have formed both the synthesis (based on market price rigidities) and the reappraisal (market quantity rigidities) as special cases, whilst accepting neither as the general theory itself.

Enough has been said to demonstrate that the synthesis does not encompass Keynes's economics, indeed the reappraisal is itself a generalization of the synthesis. But is Keynes's economics a generalization of the reappraisal? In my view, it can be so considered for the following related reasons.

First, Keynes did not restrict his analysis either to a 'quantity adjusting to price' system nor to a 'quantity adjusting to quantity' system, but envisaged that any economy would consist of a combination of markets each with varying speeds of quantity and price adjustment and interaction. This is not a particularly devastating generalization, until, secondly, it is set within the framework of enquiry that seeks to find what determines when an economy (or markets within it) change from one structure and system of adjustment to another. Why should an economy behaving more or less according to the rules of 'classical' theory suddenly be thrown into a completely different system of adjustment? Quite clearly this is something that lies outside the scope of the reappraisal, not because it relies upon the extreme system of 'quantity adjusting to quantity' alone, for this is not necessary to it, but because as a theory it is based on the aggregation of individual propensities, it would have to rely upon an exogenous shock to bring about change (whether as a change in the individual propensities or the technical conditions in which they operate). Third, Keynes was constructing a macroeconomic proper in which aggregate economic variables had a status distinguishable from their existence as a sum of the actions of individual economic agents. It is in this that Keynes quite clearly departs from the reappraisal.

On this last point, Keynes theory of expectations is of particular importance. As we have seen for his interest theory, and marginal efficiency capital, expectations occupied a central position. On the other hand, fluctuations in expectations cannot be taken for granted, to be random, or the aggregated effect of many individual decisions. Keynes referred to two sources of waves of pessimism, rejecting the notion that these depended upon a mass irrational psychology. First, the institutional development of investment markets, associated with the increasing separation of ownership and control, divorced short-run speculative profit-making from the underlying rationale of long-run production possibilities. In the Stock Exchange for example, absurd day-to-day fluctuations in shares become amplified and reverberate with disproportionate effect on the levels of income and employment. In addition, financing and entrepreneurial talent are drawn into this game of musical chairs, for within it are the greatest individual profits to be made even if on aggregate there must be losses (as investment and, through the multiplier, output, rather than chairs, are lost to the players to provide for the game itself).

Second, Keynes argued that as income grew over time there would be a tendency for the saving rate to rise and, in so far as this saving is realized as investment, a tendency for the PMEC to decline as the more productive outlets for capital are filled. Consequently, it was necessary for there to be a corresponding secular decline in the rate of interest. This would lead to the false expectation of the necessity for the rate of interest to rise above its existing (and full employment equilibrium) level, because of past experience of relatively high interest rates. The result would be the unemployment equilibrium in the shortrun that we have described above.

Keynes's recognition of the importance of the role played by the development of the social institutions organizing finance and investment implies that he locates the causes of unemployment in factors other than the aggregation of individual propensities and random shocks. He must also be given credit for recognizing that these institutional factors were not perhaps systematic enough to explain the tendency towards short-run unemployment. On the other hand, the elements of his explanation that draw upon the existence of an increasing propensity to save with income and a diminishing marginal product of capital are completely arbitrary and ahistorical. Like Ricardo, he believed that productivity would decline with accumulation, but unlike Ricardo he did not even rely upon the exhaustion of a scarce factor of production (fertile land). But, just because Keynes proved unable to theorize adequately the social conditions that tend to throw the economy into an unemployment of ineffective demand, this does not mean that others have not tried. We now turn to these attempts.

vii. Theories of Underconsumption

Not surprisingly, those theories that try to explain socially the tendency to ineffective demand draw upon an analysis of the expenditure behaviour of classes or the state. For example, Malthus praised the role of the landlord class in maintaining demand through its unproductive expenditure of rent. Our attention on classes will, however, focus on the relationship between capital and labour. As a result, the organizing principle of the theories concerned is that macro-economic aggregates should be divided according to profits and wages rather than according to consumption and investment as in the traditional multiplier model. Thus, it is generally presumed that the expenditure of profits and wages is inadequate relative to the (potential) production of profits.

In its simplest form (Kalecki, Kaldor and Pasinetti) this theory takes investment and the propensity to save of capitalists as exogenous and determines the level of profits by a simple multiplier in which profits replace national income and the capitalists' savings rate replaces that for the economy as a whole.

$$I + C = P$$

$$C = (1\text{-}s)\,P$$

$$\text{Hence } P = \frac{I}{s}$$

where P, I, C and s are capitalists' profits, investments, consumption and savings rate. National income is made up of these profits together with the wages of the number of workers necessary to produce the national income.

Now, as has been brought out, this theory is in most respects equivalent to the Keynesian theory. As such, it is subject to the same criticisms, particularly of ultimately resting upon the aggregated propensities of individuals (capitalists) to save, invest and hold money, unless alternative theories of these are brought forward. This is precisely what is done (although the Keynesian theory of money is rarely challenged) by linking the level of investment, not to the mass of profits, but to the rate of profit. As accumulation proceeds, the demand for labour increases, strengthening the working class in distributional struggle (but also in resisting capitalist discipline because of the ease of finding work), increasing wages and reducing profitability thereby precipitating a downturn. In the work of Baran and Sweezy and others, emphasis is laid upon the low level of wages as a source of ineffective demand, but this is complemented by the notion that monopoly undermines the competitive incentive to invest as an alternative source of demand. Finally, these theories tend to see the role of the state as a contradictory one, making expenditures to increase effective demand to maintain profits and employment (in response to political demands), but simultaneously thereby undermining the basis for profitable production by absorbing resources and increasing the economic strength of the working class.

viii. Critique of Keynesianism

It is of course the standard criticism of Keynesian theory from a Marxist perspective that its analysis lies rooted within the sphere of exchange. Even if it frees itself from a methodology based upon individualism, it nevertheless treats the social relations, embodied, for example, in financial institutions or the aggregate levels of profits and wages and the distributional struggle based on its division, in isolation from the class relations of production.

This criticism can be demonstrated in *structural* terms by reference to the diagram on page 20. In it the spheres of exchange and distribution are readily identified as lying between the two dotted lines. It is around these relationships, including the dealings of money-capital contained within the central M, that Keynesian theories are organized. The process of production of surplus value which lies outside this domain could just as well be absent. The one exception is Keynes's theory of the secular decline in the PMEC but this is a superficial and at best tautologous explanation of the necessity for falling profitability. Otherwise Keynes's theory is based upon the confinement of money-flows within the central M as a consequence of speculation. For the neo-classical synthesis and reappraisal, money is also hoarded because market prices or market quantities, respectively, fail to adjust. In addition, the tendency exists to fractionalize the diagram into finer and finer economic units and this is reflected in the multi-sector models or macro-econometrics.

For the other theories, in the underconsumptionist tradition, we can readily identify the various relationships that are emphasized either one at a time or in combination. A focus on the limited consuming power of workers determines the aggregate circulation of commodities (i.e. effective demand) by the purchase from sector 2 of $V_1 + V_2$, whilst the limited purchasing power of capitalists (or the state) for consumer goods focuses attention on the expenditure $S_1 + S_2$. On the other hand, the limited outlets or competitive compulsion for investment is seen to constrain the aggregate circulation of commodities according to the size of $C_1 + C_2$. Finally, the decline in profitability as workers' economic strength increases is reflected in the deficiency of $m_1 + m_2$ as the motive force of production.

The various forms of Keynesianism can also be located in terms of the various 'policy' implications to which they lead. Because Keynes himself identified the problems of deficient demand in terms of social factors, his proposals were necessarily relatively radical, calling for public investment and consumption, public control of aggregate investment and redistribution of income and wealth to increase the average propensity to consume. It was only Keynes's propensity to defend the elite privilege of entrepreneurial initiative and freedom of choice that appears to divide him from Fabian socialism (but even this doctrine included the need for meritocracy). On the other hand, the narrower scope of economic vision implied by both the neo-classical synthesis and the reappraisal necessarily leads to a more limited terrain of debate over economic policy. The management of the level of aggregate demand is controversial only in terms of the relative sequence and speeds of adjustment of the various markets and economic variables. In this light, different policy instruments concerned with, for example, the rate of interest, government expenditure and budget deficit, the money supply and taxation, are seen as effective according to their effect on aggregate demand and subsequently output and employment. Debate can be confined to these considerations, and the wider social conditions of state intervention can be safely left to the microeconomics of externalities, public goods and natural monopolies, or to the ethics of normative economics.

For the underconsumptionist theories in the radical tradition, the conclusion drawn for policy is, of course, that there is no solution within the capitalist system to the problems of deficient demand, whether met by low wages (deficient demand for consumption goods) or high wages (low profits and deficient demand for investment goods). Nevertheless, such analyses do allow an understanding of economic policy-making in terms of interventions over the level of demand through state expenditure or other measures. What is never made clear is why, in contrast to Keynesian ideology, such state economic intervention is unable to abolish crises and the co-existence of idle machinery and workers. For, whilst it must be admitted that the state cannot control the distributional struggle between classes (even if it intervenes in general on behalf of capital represented as society), it could regulate demand to ensure that erosions of profits only leads to a slackening in the pace of accumulation (i.e. unemployment of labour but not necessarily of capital).

Other than establishing new proportions between consumption and investment, a problem that is recognized by orthodox theory as frictional and structural unemployment, the underconsumptionist theories would appear to have to rely upon the speculative role played by money in desynchronizing the economy in the circumstances outlined above. This is not a surprising conclusion for underconsumptionist theories are usually silent on the role played by money, thus implicitly accepting a standard Keynesian view, or specifically see speculative activity as the simultaneous product of deficient demand.

It is this view of the role played by money or more generally the credit system that can act as a point of departure for a Marxist critique of Keynesian-based theories. For Keynes, speculative activity institutionalized for example in the Stock Exchange, was the tail that wagged the dog of productive investment. If such speculation could be confined to the casino, the potential problems of deficient demand would be very much reduced. It must be agreed that speculation is the necessary counterpart to the socialization of investment through the various institutions of the credit system, for just as this brings the separation of ownership from control, so it divorces the value of assets from their cost of reproduction and potential profitability. On the other hand, these insights should not be seen as the basis for analysing their effects but their causes. It is here that theories of effective demand are deficient because they ignore the role played by the credit system in centralizing capital as competition coerces the need for an ever-increasing minimum level of individual capital to guarantee sufficiently high levels of productivity.

Nor does this remain a criticism of the Keynesian theory of money *per se*. For to recognize the role played by money markets in centralizing capital is to forge a direct link with the class relations of production and the production of surplus value. For what centralization involves is the reorganization of workers in production, within and between (diversification) sectors in larger units as well as by the relative expulsion of living labour by the introduction of machinery. Keynesian theory at best represents this as frictional and structural unemployment in the movement to an equilibrium or from one to another. In contrast, it should be seen as a never-ending process of disequilibrium. That this credit expansion is necessary for capital accumulation as a means of centralization, does not mean that the centralization is successfully accomplished since it is not simply a financial operation but a reorganization of workers in production. In other words, speculation is the tip of the iceberg, the productive body of which is by no means guaranteed to be free from uncertainty provided the level of demand is sufficiently maintained.

But why should the accumulation process lead to crises and why can it not be analysed and controlled in terms of the Keynesian categories of aggregate demand? The general answer is that the accumulation process does not ultimately depend upon the demand generated for profitable production but upon the ability to produce profits. The control of demand and finance is not control of the accumulation process and for that reason demand and finance cannot be controlled although interventions may be made through them, increasingly by the state as capitalism matures.

To be more specific, consider a period of unemployment, the Keynesian prescription for which would be an increase in effective demand through one policy or another. In contrast, it can be argued that the increase in demand could temporarily obstruct the process of centralization through easing the liquidity problems of those firms that would otherwise be bankrupted, merged or acquired. Whether this is so or not depends upon the particular degree of development of the social mechanism for centralizing capital and the strength of resistance to the effects of reorganization by the working class.

These should not be seen as two simultaneous but independent factors. The working class will struggle over the conditions or work and the level of employment and this may, for example, be reflected in the demand for nationalization or other state economic intervention, which then are the forms in which reorganization is socially organized. Marxism's argument is, however, that accumulation increasingly intensifies class struggle and thereby over-constrains the ability to reorganize capital. But the objects and forms of resistance are not confined to struggles over the production process alone, but are given expression, for example, in terms of distributional conflict and the demand for reflation. And it is these phenomena that give radical Keynesianism the appearance of determining the real underlying processes. If we consider the level of wages, both Keynes and Marx argued that they would rise during a boom and this makes nonsense of the idea that subsequent slumps are caused by deficient consuming power due to low levels of wages. On the other hand, this view would appear to lend support to the explanation of crises based on falling profitability due to rising wages.

However, no such simple relationship between wages and profitability can be allowed, once we recognize that accumulation has as its object the increasing of productivity through centralization. For then, both profitability *and* wages can rise. Whilst it is true that accumulation leads to an increasing economic strength of the working class in distributional struggle and hence a stimulus to increasing wages, these are also the means by which labour power (variable capital) is reorganized. In other words, higher wages are the product of accumulation not simply because of distributional struggle but also because they are essential to the reorganization of production. Consequently they cannot be taken to be an exogenous cause of crises according to the strength of distributional struggle, but must be related to the pace of accumulation and centralization and the success with which it is accomplished.

ix. Concluding Remarks

The purpose of the preceding section has not been to produce an alternative theory of macro-economic aggregates as a stick with which to beat existing Keynesian theories of aggregate demand and the output and employment to which it leads. Rather it is hoped that two things have been implicitly shown. First, the construction of macro-economic aggregates in the Keynesian tradition and their integration within a macro-econometric model is a futile exercise in understanding the movement of the capitalist economy since these macro-economic aggregates are the product of forces and relationships that are excluded from the model. Second, nevertheless, macro-economics in the Keynesian tradition (and at one extreme monetarism) provides a theoretical framework in which economic policy can be formed to mediate conflicts within the capitalist class as well as conflicts with the working class. Thus, the centralization and accumulation of capital, and the cycle of production that accompanies it, is not comprehended within the framework of Keynesianism, but this theory does provide the practical ideology by which capitalism may be reproduced.

Further Reading

It is highly recommended that Keynes's *General Theory* be read first hand. On the neo-classical synthesis, see any standard macro textbook. For an introduction to the reappraisal, A Leijonhufvud, *Keynes and the Classics*, IEA Pamphlet No. 30, 1969 gives a simple introductory account. The classic modern work of underconsumptionism is P. Baran and P. Sweezy, *Monopoly Capital*, Monthly Review Press, 1964. A survey of theories is to be found in M. Bleaney, *Underconsumption Theories*, Lawrence and Wishart, 1976.

4

World Economic Crisis and Inflation

Faced with the need to understand the world economic recession we are presented with an embarrassing wealth of objects for analysis. There are the indicators of the recession itself — massive unemployment, unprecedented general levels of inflation and monetary crises. These have to be set against the conditions which characterized the post-war boom. What are the effects and significance of the growth of multi-national corporations (MNCs), the increasing economic interventions of the state, the development of social democracy, the changing forms of imperialism, etc? The problem is to extract from these phenomena those that are decisive and around which a general explanation can be organized. This is done in the following sections. There, we will neither deal with the significance of inflation as a cause nor as a consequence of the current recession. In the next nine sections, this will be done for bourgeois theory, where it will be shown that the current coexistence of inflation and recession is explained according to the role played by expectations. In the last two sections, the bourgeois theory will be criticized by offering an alternative framework for analysing inflation which draws upon the understanding of the recession presented in the first section.

i. Capital, Monopoly and the State

Capitalism, like all modes of production, is composed of a set of social relations of production upon which is built a superstructure of political and ideological relations. For capitalism to continue in existence its reproduction must be guaranteed and this requires that class struggle at all levels be contained within definite limits.[1] This is accomplished *as much* by the forms and objects that the inevitable class struggle is encouraged and induced to take *as* the relative strength of antagonistic classes. Even successful struggles by the working class can leave the fundamental relations of capitalist production untouched. Nevertheless, the development of capitalist production still requires changes in the relations of production, whilst the capital-labour relation remains. As a result, the accompanying superstructure and the forms and objects of class struggle will be transformed also. This process, however, should not be seen as an automatic and harmonious evolution, but one in which class struggle obstructs capitalist development unless there is a development of the relations of production, and even then class struggle propels capitalism forward to new conflicts.

So far, however, we have made no reference to the very motive of capitalist production — the thirst for profit. Historically, at its origins, capitalism satisfied this thirst by crude and oppressive methods utilizing the existing methods of production and exploiting them (or more exactly workers) to the full. As capitalism develops, machinery begins to replace the tasks undertaken by the labourer in production and more raw materials are worked up in a given time. Simultaneously, the growth of large-scale manufacture allows the productivity of cooperation, scale, and division of labour to be utilized. With these developments, class struggle focuses on unemployment (as workers are displaced and deskilled by the productivity of machinery) and working conditions (as machinery forces a new pace and division of labour). With increasing scale of production, workers are organized in larger and larger numbers at the point of production. Whilst the capitalist purpose in this is the pursuit of profit, the workers' material interests are represented by the formation of trade unions, the organizational conditions for which are created by capitalist production itself.

The accumulation of capital brings with it capital's developed laws of motion. We have already implicitly argued that the pursuit of profit leads to an increase in the minimum level of capital necessary to achieve the levels of productivity that competition forces on the production process. Clearly, the more capital that can metaphorically speaking, be collected into the control of a single hand the better. The means by which this monopolization of capital can best take place is through the credit system (as illustrated by the development of the British financial system in the late nineteenth century). The funds of capitalists in general can be made available to a few capitalists in particular. This accomplishes what might be called a financial restructuring of capital, but it only creates the potential restructuring of capital in production. As we have already briefly seen this involves a development of the relations of production and this is tempered by class struggle over the implications of restructuring capitalist production. There are the effects on individual work-places: unemployment at those small-scale factories that are closed down as inefficient, relative or even absolute falls in employment at those factories that are expanded, with speed-up and deskilling for those who remain employed. Besides these and governed by them are the effects in society as a whole. Whatever the pace of accumulation, it requires the centralization or restructuring of capital in production. Consequently, there is a permanent pool of unemployed formed by those who are thrown out of work by closure or displacement by machinery. This pool is an important element in restructuring workers in prt duction, for capital can draw on its reserves to fill the places that are created in expanding factories and impose a new discipline on them and the existing workforce more readily.

Restructuring of capital is also essentially an uneven process. Sectors of production expand at different rates and with different rhythms. Production tends to become concentrated in specific areas leading to overdevelopment in some instances and decay in others. Historically, this uneven development proved itself in the form of the separation between expanding cities and the depopulated country. Now, it has application to the widening differentials between regions and countries.

These effects of restructuring are resisted by the workers, organized into trade unions. Whilst the credit system proves a powerful lever in financial restructuring, capital's offensive to reorganize the relations of production are limited to the market forces of economic compulsion and the ideological and political power that belongs to the ruling class. The mechanisms of reorganization prove incapable of accommodating an accumulating capital, that not only produces the effects of centralization that we have already discussed but also requires the continued production of profits. At times, the pressures to expand capital and satisfy the motive of profit-making prove incompatible, and the economy suffers a sharp financial crisis followed by recession.

Recessions are characterized by the coexistence of idle workers and machinery. Both in turn intensify capital's economic compulsion to reorganization. Unemployed workers are essentially unorganized and can be more easily disciplined and reabsorbed into the process of production dictated by capital. But recessions also destroy capitals, weeding out the weak and inefficient and allowing their resources to be centralized through bankruptcy, acquisition and merger. Consequently, recessions are an expression of capital's limited ability to be reorganized, but are also a powerful force behind renewed reorganization. It is this that explains why capitalist accumulation does not proceed smoothly, but is punctuated by crises and recessions, giving rise to a cycle of production that is fundamentally a cycle of restructuring and destruction of capital.

However, it is not simply the relations of production that are reorganized through the process of production, the means of reorganization are themselves developed. This we have already discussed briefly in relation to the credit system. Here, the creation of a banking system allows financial restructuring to be accomplished more readily. Large-scale banks give rise to large-scale corporations and monopoly capital develops alongside and as a product of finance capital. It is the consolidation of the phenomena just discussed that gives rise to the period of *monopoly capitalism*. As we have seen, monopoly capitalism is to be associated with new objects of class struggle — over unemployment, deskilling, speed-up of work — and new forms of struggle as the working class is organized into trade unions.

Capital accumulation is beset by crises that are intensified by the growing strength of working-class struggle. It becomes increasingly impossible to confine the effects of these crises to economic reproduction as the working class seeks the political rights and the exercise of political power to defend and advance its economic interests. Out of these conflicts within monopoly capitalism develops the stage of state monopoly capitalism SMC, characteristic of the current post World War II period. Fundamental to this stage of capitalism is the increasing economic role played by the state. But this role must be seen relative to the cycle of restructuring that is fundamental to capital accumulation. The state does not intervene to control or abolish the cycle but to promote it and moderate its effects on social reproduction. Consider this a little further.

In bourgeois economic theory, state economic intervention is usually divided according to the division of the theory itself into macro- and micro-economics. As a result, the role of the state in the discussion of growth and recession is usually restricted to considerations of Keynesian aggregate demand. Conversely, the role of the state in its policies towards nationalized industries, for example, is usually confined to considerations of micro-economic efficiency in the context of partial equilibrium and an otherwise fully employed economy. By contrast, our emphasis here is on the relationship between the state and the expansion where possible of capital accumulation. The state's role in capitalist society is primarily to guarantee *social* reproduction in general, to create cohesion and stability in political and ideological relations despite the antagonisms produced within these by the class nature of society and the disruptions accompanying capitalist accumulation in its economic reproduction. On the other hand private capital as such is only concerned directly with its own individual economic reproduction (buying, producing and selling for profit) and this explains the necessity for the existence of the capitalist state.

Once the state makes economic interventions, it can act as a force to moderate the conflicts associated with the accumulation of capital, as it widens its responsibility for guaranteeing social reproduction. Policies are developed oriented towards the level of employment, wages, etc.

The state's clearest intervention into the accumulation of capital is where it takes control of production itself — nationalization. Here, together with its policies of aid, subsidy and supervision to

Table 1

	Taxation as a Percentage of GNP	
	1929	1974
CANADA	7.3	39.7
DENMARK	7.9	53.4
FRANCE	10.3	41.1
NETHERLANDS	11.4	50.6
NORWAY	8.4	52.9
SWEDEN	7.4	49.1
UK	17.5	38.7
USA	4.6	32.0 (1973)

private industry, its policies are generally directed towards a restructuring into large-scale profitable production. But the state also intervenes in exchange processes, becoming itself a dominant agent of credit, whether through its overall policies of 'demand management' or in its granting of loans to particular firms or industries. Intervention in distributional struggle between classes takes the form of incomes policy, and in addition taxation becomes a significant means by which profits are redistributed through the state as well as financing state expenditure.

However, state economic intervention must not be understood as the state simply acting as a surrogate for private capital. For, the state's economic interventions must have the effect of moderating the intensified crises associated with monopoly capitalism. On the other hand, the more intimate is the link between the state and economic reproduction, the greater are the potential political and ideological conflicts produced by conflicts over economic issues. The struggles for wages and employment increasingly become struggles within and potentially against the state.

As a result a political transformation is a prerequisite of state economic intervention. Typically, this takes the form of social democracy which has the effect of integrating the struggles of the labour movement into the state apparatus in correspondence to the state's economic interventions on behalf of capital. This is not simply an ideological necessity for capitalism (although this is important), allowing the state to represent its role in continuing capital accumulation as actions in the interests of society as a whole. More important, the struggles of the working class may be divorced from its point of strength and organization — in the process of production — and be conducted through democratic channels where it will be weakened.

Now, the creation of social democracy is not essential for the state to be able to make the economic interventions — an alternative is a fascist dictatorship. But if social democracy is established, and this will depend upon a successful working-class political struggle, working-class economic struggles will take new forms and have more immediate and direct political implications. This is because these struggles become articulated through the state. In the case of employment, workers struggle for state intervention to maintain jobs through struggles for nationalization, import controls and aid to the industry concerned. As we have already seen, the satisfaction of these demands can be compatible with the continued promotion of capitalist accumulation. But it would be a mistake therefore to identify these struggles, limited to reformism though they may be, with the interests of capital as opposed to workers.

For the working class will struggle to force the state to intervene in production in its interest as opposed to that of capital which remains the production of profit through the reorganization and accumulation of capital. This is clear in so far as the struggle develops for workers' control and the orientation of production for the maintenance of employment, the improvement of working conditions and the production of output according to the criterion of social use as opposed to profitable sale.

ii. The World Economy

The significance of and stimulus to state economic intervention cannot be understood in isolation from developments in the world economy. State economic intervention and the internationalization of capital together serve as a focus for understanding the post-war boom as well as the crisis that has followed it on a world scale.

For, it we contrast the post-war period with the inter-war period the importance of these developments stands out sharply. In the earlier period state economic intervention was severely limited (except in the case of the Fascist powers, where the political implications of state economic interventions could be suppressed).

Of course, the internationalization of capital has developed from the very beginnings of capitalism with the tendency to create a world market. But up to the Second World War, this was still restricted to competition between capitals on the basis of the imperialist division of the world into spheres of influence for the export of finance and commodities. After the Second World War, and associated with it the emergence of the dominance of American capitalism, new conditions for the international expansion of capitalism were created. Interpenetration of capitals between the advanced economies displaced the importance of the intensive exploitation of empires. This is reflected in the changing patterns of trade and investment in the world economy.

However, more is involved than a simple quantitative shift in the orientation of trade and investment. In particular, a new form of internationalizing capital has emerged, one that is only possible once the classic division of the world into economic empires has been broken down. It involves the internationalization of the pro-

Table 2

Value of World Trade		
	1929	1973
Between Developed Areas	23.9	63.8
Between Underdeveloped Areas	12.0	4.3
Between Developed and Underdeveloped Areas	62.6	32.0

Table 3 Percentage Distribution of Accumulated US and UK Foreign Investment (Still in aggregate more than 70 per cent of World Foreign Investment in 1973)

		Developed Areas	Underdeveloped Areas
US	1929	50.7	49.3
	1973	76.4	23.6
UK	1930	53.1	46.9
	1973	72.1	27.9

cess of production itself. By this is meant the organization of production within a single firm across national boundaries so that, for example, parts may be manufactured in one or more countries but be assembled in another country and finally be sold on the world market. The 'factory' of the MNC increasingly straddles national boundaries, although data illustrating this on an aggregate level are difficult to obtain.

Table 4 Number and Distribution of Affiliates of MNCs (two affiliates in one country counts once) 1968/69.

'Home' Country	Affiliates	Percentage Developed	Located Underdeveloped
United States	9691	74.7	25.3
United Kingdom	7116	68.2	31.8
World	27300	73.6	26.4

Nor is the internationalization of production expanded at the expense of the internationalization of other forms of capital. The figures on international liquidity illustrate the increasing role of international finance, the increasing state intervention into credit relations as reflected by the expansion of paper money, but also the growth of supranational economic organizations.

Table 5 Internationalization of Production in the Motor Car Industry (1975)

Firm	Number of Foreign Affiliates Involved in Production	Number Assembling Only
Chrysler	12	5
General Motors	21	16
Renault	23	22
Volkswagen	6	3
British Leyland	43	38
Fiat	23	18
Ford	21	18

Table 6 International Liquidity

	1929		1976	
	$b	%	$b	%
Gold	10.2	69	42	18
Currency Assets	4.5	31	166	70
IMF and Special Drawing Rights	—	—	28	12

The data on world trade show its growth relative to world production.

Table 7 Growth in World Trade and Production

Volume Index	1963	1972
Exports	100	213
Manufacturing Production	100	123
Primary Production	100	165

iii. The Current Economic Recession

The foregoing analysis has argued that the two most important developments of the post-war period are the growth of state economic intervention and the internationalization of capital, particularly for the latter the internationalization of productive capital as a point of departure from earlier periods. Consequently any general understanding of the laws of development of capitalism, for example, as presented in earlier sections, must have a specific application to capitalism's current development with these characteristics in mind. In these terms, the post-war world economy can be seen as developing an accumulation in the form of state economic intervention and internationalization. More, these are the means by which accumulation was promoted. Consequently, it is not surprising that the post-war period should have witnessed a long-period of expansion for the world economy, as the new forces underlying that expansion permitted and fed a massive accumulation and reorganization of capital on a world scale.

But why should such an expansion collapse into recession? The answer is to be found in general terms in the increasing incompatibility of the internationalization of capital with state economic intervention. Not that these tendencies are necessarily incompatible, for the state often adopts policies to promote the internationalization of capital. Rather, it is the growing class resistance to these developments that eventually undermines the expansion. For because the *state* intervenes to internationalize capital, that internationalization becomes restricted by the state's more fundamental role of guaranteeing social reproduction. But, because the state *internationalizes* capital, social reproduction within the nation becomes restricted by the needs of international economic reproduction. As capital is accumulated and class struggle intensifies, it is these conflicts between the needs of social and economic reproduction that come to the fore in the current period of capitalism.

To capture the characteristics of capital's international expansion, many theorists and particularly Marxists following Lenin have coined the term imperialism. So far we have shown that the tendency towards SMC is an ambiguous development as far as imperialist expansion is concerned, at times obstructing and at times promoting the internationalization of capital by its economic interventions and moderation of wider social conflicts. As a result, it is hardly surprising that the extent of state economic intervention is unevenly distributed from country to country, according to the extent that each state is forced to moderate class conflict through economic interventions on the one hand and to the extent that MNCs can internationalize their operations unaided on the other.

More specifically, workers' struggles become directed through the state against the effects of international capitalist accumulation. They are oriented towards employment, welfare or incomes policy, they create an increasing tension between the fundamental need for economic reproduction in the form of capital accumulation and restructuring and the need for social reproduction and the moderation of economic as well as political and ideological struggle. These conflicts are more pronounced the more capital is internationalized since working-class struggle to defend its economic interests through the state increasingly obstructs the internationalization of capital. Further, these struggles cannot be simply resolved by a transfer of capital abroad because they involve through the state the question of the stability of capitalist society as well as of the economy. In short, the development of SMC has not abolished the cycles of production associated with capital accumulation (as Keynesian theory focusing on the management of effective demand would argue) but has given them a new form of existence. The state through its economic policies may temper the rhythm and intensity of recessions and the social conflicts to which they give rise. But it does so at the expense of transforming economic struggles so that they have immediate political implications with the result that the free development of capital's international expansion founders on working-class economic and political resistance.

So far, we have attempted to show two things. First, why it is that the development of capitalism should give rise to the increasing role of the state in economic intervention together with the internationalization of capital in production. Second, why these developments should have given rise to the post-war boom but nevertheless lead to a recession. In the final part of this section, it remains to examine the course that the recession takes in the light of this analysis.

The current recession, like all those that have preceded it, has the function for capital of laying the foundation for a renewed accumulation by restructuring existing capital. Now, however, this restructuring has the peculiar symptoms of being oriented towards the internationalization of productive capital stimulated by state economic intervention. In addition, the state's interventions have the effect of moderating the social implications of the economic conflicts generated by the recession (often implemented through state economic policy), whether these concern struggles over employment, or the levels of real wages and welfare services as these are cut to redistribute profits to capital.

In some instances, the growing strength of class struggle and its expression politically has not only precipitated recession but has also led to profound changes in social organization. Within Europe, there have been crises in the dictatorships of Spain, Portugal and Greece. In the underdeveloped countries, the complex interaction of the tendencies we have identified coexist through imperialist exploitation with backward capitalist and even pre-capitalist relations of production. As has been seen in Africa, Latin America and elsewhere, the process of capital accumulation, leading to reorganization through recession, generates the necessity for sweeping social change. In each case, the result is not necessarily defeats for the working classes, the precondition of a renewed accumulation. Rather, objectively posed is the necessity for seizure of power by a working people committed to a socialist transformation of the relations in which they produce and live.

iv. The Pre-Keynesian Quantity Theory of Inflation

It is perhaps appropriate both logically and historically to begin a summary of bourgeois inflation theory with the quantity theory of money.[2] As proposed by Fisher, the equation $Mv = pT$ relates the supply of money M, the price level p, and the number of transactions undertaken T to the velocity of circulation v. As such, the velocity of circulation simply represents the efficiency of institutional arrangements for making transactions. On the other hand, in the almost identical Cambridge equation of the demand for money $M_d = kpY$ the transactions demand for money M_d is related to the desired ratio of cash balances to money income. The condition for equilibrium in the money market, $M_s = M_d = kpY$, readily transforms into the determination of the price level $p = \frac{M}{kY}$. From this it follows that the rate of increase of the price level (the rate of inflation) equals the rate of increase of the money supply since the two are proportional for given k and Y. Despite the fact, as we shall see, that economic theory has long since rejected this crude form of the quantity theory, it still remains a popular means of explaining inflation, summarized in the slogan 'too much money chasing too few goods'. The reason for this is in part due to the structure of the argument which has survived even if with modification. The focus on the equalization of the demand for money to an exogenously determined supply almost inevitably leads to a theory of the expansion of the money supply as a cause of inflation.

For, whatever variables the demand for money is assumed to depend upon other than income and the price level, these are hardly liable to be considered to change sufficiently to absorb the increased money supply, if inflation does occur. Consequently, whenever there is inflation some form of the quantity theory or monetary explanation is bound to be proposed as in the modern monetarism associated with Friedman and his followers.

So far we have only discussed the rate of inflation in terms of comparative statics, that is the association of a higher price level in equilibrium for a higher money supply. But inflation is a dynamic process and raises the question of the transition from one equilibrium price level to another, and also, if inflation is to be maintained, the mechanisms that lead from a continuously increasing money supply to a continuously increasing price level (for constant k and Y or at least for these rising at a slower combined rate than the money supply). The most obvious link between the formulation of static equilibrium and dynamic change in this context is through the excess demand for goods. Increase in the money supply leads to an increase in the demand for goods which cannot be met at the full employment equilibrium so that prices rise. In addition, wages (and other incomes) must rise to restore the equilibrium conditions equating relative marginal products to relative factor prices etc., otherwise there would be excess demands in these markets also.

It follows that in the adjustment process, it is not simply the money market but potentially all markets that move out of equilibrium. This may appear to be of little significance given the eventual restoration of full-employment equilibrium. However, even if we accept the neo-classical version of the neutrality of money in the determination of equilibrium (except for the level of *absolute* prices), it follows that scope exists for economic policy to intervene to influence the path and speed of adjustment to equilibrium.

Of course, it could be argued that the government should not have increased the money supply in the first place (if this rather than a reduction in k or Y is the source of inflation), and that laissez-faire is the best policy as far as the process of adjustment is concerned. But, clearly, the last proposition cannot be deduced from an inspection of the quantity equation alone, only from an understanding of the workings of the economy as a whole.

v. The Keynesian Theory of Inflation

The problem of adjustment, however, takes on even greater significance if we reject the neo-classical (and classical) notion of the neutrality of money in determining equilibrium, and recognize the possibility, as in Keynesian theory, of the existence of unemployment equilibrium brought about by the interaction of the money and real markets. For then, it is not simply a question of increases in the money supply leading, according to the demand for money function, to the same real equilibrium at a different (inflated) price level, with only the path and speed of adjustment to worry about. It is possible that a new, even full employment, vquilibrium may be established without any increases in prices at all.

The reasoning underlying such a theory will almost certainly be familiar to the reader in terms of the IS-LM model. Restricting ourselves to the determination of equilibrium alone first and not arguing about movement between equilibria, it is well known that if prices (and/or wages) are sticky downwards then the desire to hold real cash balances *and* make sufficient real purchases may be thwarted by an inadequate money supply. Consequently, from the resulting unemployment equilibrium (in which the lack of money is partially reflected in lack of demand) a full employment equilibrium can be achieved by expanding the money supply without leading to inflation. The demand for and supply of money are brought into equilibrium by an expansion of output[3] In the IS-LM model, if the LM curve cannot be shifted to the right by a fall in prices to achieve full-employment equilibrium, then it can be shifted by an increase in the money supply. As a result the Keynesian model demonstrates that an expansion of the money supply does not lead to inflation as long as there is not full employment.

vi. The Keynesian 'Inflationary Gap'

By the same token, however, the model does give rise to inflation for expansion of the money supply over and above the level necessary to achieve full employment. Consider first the Keynesian theory of the inflationary gap. If we construct the overall level of demand (expenditure) from the consumption function and autonomously given levels of investment and government expenditure, then in aggregate this may exceed full employment output, the difference constituting the inflationary gap.[4] The outcome is supposedly an increase in the level of prices that reduces the real level of money expenditures to the level of full employment output.

As it stands, this Keynesian explanation of inflation appears to be independent of the money market, no reference has been made to the supply of and demand for money. This is a result of the simplicity and incompleteness of the model. To begin with investment is taken as exogenous and independent of the rate of interest. Secondly, if the inflationary gap is closed when prices rise, this presupposes a consumption function based on money rather than real income otherwise as prices rise so would consumption expenditures in proportion. When the inflationary gap is closed, some proportion of the originally intended real consumption and investment must be decreased (leaving aside government expenditure) and this can only be done in a fuller model including a money market influenced by the rate of interest.[5] In fact, the simple inflationary gap model corresponds to the simple multiplier model. Just as this needs to be elaborated into the IS-LM model to incorporate an endogenous determination of investment, so the same applies to the Keynesian theory of inflation.

At this point, it is necessary to consider then the Keynesian demand for money function. It is generally given in the form $M_d = pf(Y, r)$. The introduction of the interest rate r into the demand for money can be justified by a number of reasons. First, the rate of interest represents the interest foregone by holding money for whatever purpose (whether transactions or precautionary). Second, money may be held for speculative purposes. In particular, the lower (higher) is the rate of interest the higher (lower) it may be *expected* to be, giving rise to plans to purchase bonds later (now) at a lower price than otherwise.[6] For our purposes, the introduction of the rate of interest in the demand for money is not so important as the introduction of expectations. For it is these which can explain the market rigidities that give rise to unemployment and inflation, as we shall see. If neo-classical economics introduced the rate of interest into the demand for money without introducing a theory of expectations, then in the absence of market rigidities, its full employment propositions coupled with the neutrality of money would continue to hold as for the quantity theory.

However, when we elaborate the inflationary-gap model into the IS-LM framework, the results are not substantially changed. Up to full employment, an increase in the money supply will expand output. Above full employment, the price level will increase in proportion to the increase in the money supply. There are, however, two exceptions. For the case of a vertical IS curve, in which investment is assumed to be independent of the interest rate, employment cannot be increased by shifts of the LM curve. An increase in the money supply is dissipated in a fall in the rate of interest with no effect on investment at (or below) full employment. As such, this corresponds to a rigidity in the workings of the investment market which can only be 'explained' by assuming investment is exogenous. On the other hand, in the case of the liquidity trap, in which the LM curve is horizontal, there is no similar rigidity in the money market. The increase in the money supply is simply held by individuals and not spent, in the expectation of increasing interest rates, so that the rate of interest is not reduced stimulating aggregate demand and inflation at full employment (or output at below full employment). What we have shown within the Keynesian framework, with the introduction of a modified demand for money function in which expectations play a role, is that inflation can only occur for the expansion of aggregate demand (for example, but not necessarily, through an expansion of the money supply) above full employment levels.[7] This is a necessary but not a sufficient condition for inflation, since expectations can give rise to a liquidity trap for which aggregate demand cannot expand. Nevertheless, inflation can only be sustained, in the absence of other exogenous increases in (government) expenditure, by increases in the money supply.

So far, within the Keynesian framework, we have only considered the different possible equilibria. We have not investigated the movement between equilibria. It has been presumed that an increase in the money supply results in an expansion of aggregate demand and this leads to an expansion of output below full employment, for example, because the new equilibrium demands this. However, the actual movement of the economy from this original equilibrium may not follow this direction of movement, and, if it does, it may not do so fast enough. Consequently, an increase in the money supply may lead to inflation in the short run if prices respond to excess demand prior to the expansion of output. Consequently, whilst the equilibrium analysis may not be in dispute, different views can be generated about the relative merits of monetary as opposed to fiscal policy for achieving the desired full employment equilibrium without too dilatory or dangerous a path of adjustment. These depend for their differences upon the relative speed and size of adjustment of prices and quantities and also the particular sequence of repercussion from one market to another. The more emphasis is given to the speed and size of adjustment of prices as opposed to quantities, the more likely is inflation in the short run. The same conclusion may be drawn, if it is presumed that goods and labour markets react more quickly than the markets tending to reduce the interest rate and increase investment.[8]

vi. The Phillips Curve

The outstanding deficiency of the Keynesian theory so far elaborated is its inability to explain the coexistence of unemployment and inflation, and more seriously the simultaneous rise in the rates of inflation and unemployment characteristic of the current recession. In particular, the theoretical and practical crisis of Keynesianism can be expressed in the following terms. If unemployment is a symptom of deficient demand and if inflation is a symptom of excess demand leading to price increases, then there is the inconsistent coexistence of deficient and excess demand.

The most well known response to this problem has been the Phillips Curve. Originally, it was observed that there existed an inverse relationship between the rate of wage increases and the level of unemployment. How could this be explained theoretically? First, it is presumed that there is a positive relationship between the rate of wage increase and excess demand for labour. Wages rise faster the greater is the demand for labour relative to the supply. Second, it is presumed that there is an equilibrium level of unemployment corresponding to the frictions in the labour market. There will always be workers streaming in and out of jobs, but at this equilibrium the number of unemployed will correspond exactly to the number of vacancies on offer. The excess demand for labour will be zero (and not negative despite the existence of unemployment which significantly is 'voluntary'). Above the equilibrium level of unemployment, however, at a low level of demand for output, the level of unemployment will exceed the number of vacancies. Conversely, for low levels of unemployment, at times of excess demand for output, the number of vacancies will exceed the level of unemployment. All in all, it can be seen that there is an inverse relation between the level of excess demand for labour, measured by the number of vacancies relative to the number of unemployed, and the level of unemployment itself.

Now the level of unemployment is inversely related to the excess demand for labour, and the excess demand for labour is positively related to the rate of wage increases. It follows that the rate of wage increases is itself inversely related to the level of unemployment. Further, at the so-called natural rate of frictional unemployment at which the excess demand for labour is zero (vacancies equals unemployment), the rate of wage inflation is zero.[9] At higher levels of unemployment wages will fall, but they will rise at higher levels of unemployment. This yields a theoretical explanation of the Phillips Curve, see diagram 4.1. Further, it can be argued that the trade-off between the level of unemployment and the rate of increase in money wages is equivalent to a trade-off between unemployment and inflation (in the absence of money-illusion) as relative marginal productivities etc. are equated to the appropriate relative prices.

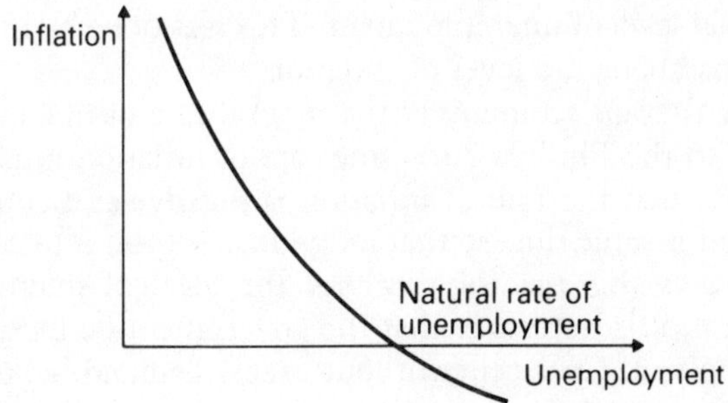

Diagram 4.1

As it stands, the Phillips curve theory does purport to explain the coexistence of inflation and unemployment. But it does so in a way that is not so much consistent as identical to the Keynesian inflationary gap approach. The major innovation is simply the argument that full employment is attained at a natural level of frictional unemployment. If aggregate demand is expanded above that level associated with the natural rate of unemployment, then employment will be increased only under the penalty of generating inflation. From the policy point of view, the government has the choice, or is under pressure, to reduce the level of unemployment but must offset any gains from this against the resulting inflation.

Nevertheless, the Phillips curve as such is still unable to explain the simultaneous increase in unemployment and the rate of inflation unless by the suggestion that the natural rate of unemployment increases for institutional reasons. This would lead to a higher rate of inflation than previously for any given level of unemployment (for example, a positive rate of inflation at the earlier natural level of unemployment). However, as it is more or less impossible to argue that frictions in the labour market steadily increase over time, the existence of increasing inflation and unemployment would appear to invalidate empirically the statistical and theoretical justification for the Phillips curve.

Paradoxically, the theory of the Phillips curve was the result of a response to a statistical relationship. When the statistical relationship broke down, the corresponding theory was not rejected but modified to explain endogenously the shifts in the (no longer existing) Phillips curve corresponding to the necessary increase in the frictional level of unemployment. This was done by introducing expectations about the level of inflation.

Consider first an economy at the natural rate of unemployment. According to the Phillips curve the rate of inflation must be zero. But suppose that the rate of inflation is positive and constant and has been so for some time so that individuals expect it to continue to be so. How is this possible without the level of unemployment falling? First, it is necessary that the government be increasing the money supply at 3 per cent without excess demand being created. Second, this occurs if 'contracts' (wage and price setting) are fixed at *expected real* levels in anticipation of inflation, as surely they will be. Putting the argument another way, if inflation exists and is anticipated at the equilibrium level of unemployment, the level of real demand and employment can only be maintained by the government by expanding the money supply to fund anticipated and contracted wage and price increases. In other words, the Phillips curve is shifted up by an amount equal to the (expected) rate of inflation.

This is hardly a surprising result in the light of the Keynesian inflationary gap approach. Remembering that the natural rate of unemployment corresponds to full employment, let us consider the aggregate level of demand when there is inflation by modifying the demand for money function to include anticipated inflation.

$M_d = pf(Y,r,r^*,i^*)$ where i is the rate of inflation and * denotes expectations. Now the higher i^* is, the less money will be held since the cost of holding money is not only the interest foregone but the erosion of purchasing power. Better to buy now than at a future higher price. The less money is held the more is spent on goods and services, which at full employment cannot be produced so that the expected inflation is self-fulfilling. Moreover, if the money supply were held constant whilst i^* remained the expected rate of inflation then there would be a temporary excess demand for money resulting in a reduction of real demand in part (and of real money balances also) and an increase in unemployment. Until the deflationary monetary policy brought the expected rate of inflation down to zero, higher levels of unemployment than the natural rate would be associated with positive rates of inflation.

So far, we have more or less restricted the analysis to the possibility of inflation at the natural rate of unemployment. Now suppose that the government attempts to maintain unemployment below the natural rate by expanding aggregate demand. Previously we would have argued from the Phillips curve that the result would have been a constant rate of inflation of say 3 per cent to close the inflationary gap. But if this 3 per cent inflation is anticipated aggregate real demand will be increased as (expected) depreciating money balances are run down. The result is a further increase in inflation, and a further upward revision of price expectations unless the government abandons its (over) employment policy and no longer funds the self-fulfilling spiral of inflationary expectations. The cycle then repeats itself leading to an accelerating inflation. Also, as we have seen earlier, to return the economy to the appropriate level of unemployment without maintaining inflation, for some period at least, unemployment will have to rise above the natural level. Within this framework, accelerating inflation and increasing unemployment can be explained in the short run if the government increases the money supply but at a rate slower than the expected rate of inflation, provided that sufficient expected real balances are held to reduce aggregate real demand. If the government does however attempt to maintain employment levels by expanding the money supply at the prevailing rate of inflation, then inflation will be accelerated.[10]

vii. Monetarist and Keynesian Theories of Inflation

It will probably not have escaped the reader that the modification of the Phillips curve presented above, to take account of expectations leads to conclusions associated with monetarist theory. On the other hand, it has been presented in such a way that it is has been linked directly with the Keynesian theory of the inflationary gap. Does this mean that monetarist and Keynesian theories of inflation and macro-economics are more or less identical?

The answer is essentially in the affirmative. Earlier we argued that the dispute between monetary and fiscal policy was based on a shared theoretical framework, the differences lying in the structure and sequence of adjustment involved in the conflicting models. Hardly surprisingly, exactly the same applies when the Keynesian framework is supplemented with hypotheses concerning expectations. The Keynesian dispute with monetarism then does not concern the explanation of inflation per se, but only the structural, sequential and quantitative role played by the individual parts. More specifically, Keynesians in general anticipate that quantities are more responsive than prices to exogenous and endogenous changes. Consequently, less emphasis is laid upon the need for severe monetary policy to restore full employment without inflation, and more emphasis is laid upon deficiencies in output rather than excesses in demand as the source of accelerating unemployment and inflation. Thus, it is not a question of the influences at work, but simply of their relative strengths.

These of course are to be estimated statistically. It cannot be overemphasized that such estimations hardly represent tests of or between the theories. On the one hand, inflation and unemployment can be distributed between the unobservable expectations and excess demand respectively according to the specification of the model. On the other hand, each model can be made sufficiently flexible to accommodate any empirical movement in macro-economic aggregates. However, there is a technical reason why monetarist theory should gain an upper hand, (as well as its popular appeal and association with right-wing laissez-faire policy-making). Because increases in the price level and money supply have co-existed, it is quite clearly easier to build and estimate macro-econometric models in the monetarist tradition than any other. Monetarists, therefore, have a built in bias, favouring their theory based on a stable demand for money function, which more or less automatically predicts a one-to-one correspondence between increases in the money supply and inflation.

ix. Cost-Push and Demand-Pull

Whilst we have shown that the monetarist and Keynesian theories share the same Keynesian theoretical presuppositions, this has necessarily led to an approach to inflation centred around excess demand and consequently so-called demand-pull factors. But just as these factors, particularly in terms of the over-expansion of the money supply, give rise to popular conceptions of the cause of inflation, so do explanations based on so-called cost-push factors. The underlying idea involved here is that particular groups commanding receipt of economic resources attempt to push up their real share by pushing up their monetary revenue. Whether one group leads the others by attempting to increase its share whilst the others simply defend their own shares,[11] or whether all groups simultaneously push to increase their shares in a redistributional conflict, the outcome is a spiral of inflation. The net outcome in real terms may in fact leave all shares unchanged, but the cake to be divided will be that much smaller because of the costs of inflation (on which see below).

Now not surprisingly, cost-push theories of inflation have also been dubbed conflict theories. Overall, we can identify three groups commonly seen as being involved in conflict, labour represented by trade unions, capital represented by monopolies, and the government represented by itself. Clearly trade unions wish to push up wages and monopolies wish to push up prices to increase their distributive shares. The government, however, simply wishes to remain in office, and is seen as doing so by acting in its interests (usually identified with labour),[12] either by maintaining or expanding the level of employment or by maintaining or expanding the level of social services (particularly immediately prior to elections after which it is under less pressure to increase its popularity).

Having identified our conflicting groups, the various theories of cost-push inflation are open to us. We simply need to choose a starting group for the vicious circle of inflating claims and allow the other groups to respond accordingly. For example, trade unions push up wages, monopolies respond by a defensive mark-up of prices to maintain profits and the government expands the money supply to ratify these changes otherwise allowing an unpopular increase in the rate of unemployment. Alternatively, the government prints money to expand popular social services, stimulating inflation and the defence of real wages and prices.

The glaring deficiency of cost-push theories of inflation is their failure to construct a theory of aggregate demand and/or output and employment. What is the size of the cake over which the various groups struggle let alone the level of prices through which distribution actually takes place? Cost-push theories only look at the supply side, whereas demand-pull theories in their developed form consider both the level of aggregate demand and the supply of factors in markets for which inflation is anticipated (the supply of labour, for example). As a result, recent developments in inflation theory tend to reject the dichotomy between cost-push and demand-pull, rather emphasizing the interaction of supply and demand. The precise nature of this interaction forms the controversy between monetarism and Keynesianism within the Keynesian framework to which we have already referred in the previous section.

Thus, cost-push and demand-pull theories of inflation are not seen as alternatives but as complements. The Phillips curve could as well be explained by the increasing distributional strength in struggle by labour as the level of employment rises, a struggle intensified in the case of anticipated inflation. But this would only investigate the supply curve for labour, and unless it is to be argued that the economy is always on the supply curve, the interacting effects of inflation on demand must also be considered.

There is no doubt that cost-push theories of inflation are as one-sided as the quantity theory of money that began our investigation into inflation. Consequently, these theories must also be integrated into the Keynesian paradigm. This having been done, they have suffered against the benchmark of tests of and within that paradigm. This is hardly surprising. First, the growth of unemployment will act statistically against models that focus predominantly on cost-push. Logically, this cannot render them 'invalid' provided an appropriate model is built that assigns inflation to the supply side and unemployment to the demand side. Secondly, however, cost-push models involve the construction of statistics appropriate to the measurement of 'pushfullness'. As these are notoriously vague (for example, how to measure union militancy) and difficult to construct, less effort has been made to justify cost-push than demand-pull oriented models of inflation.

The demise of the influence of cost-push factors in the study of inflation has had the wider implication of putting aside 'non-economic' and 'institutional' changes in the explanation of inflation. This has certainly lent support to monetarist explanations of inflation, particularly those emphasizing that the existence of trade unions (or other monopolies) can only redistribute employment or wages within the working class but otherwise have little or no effect upon the overall equilibrium attained. Again, however, such extreme views do not have to be adopted and the existence of market power and the exercise of it can be theorised to have aggregate as well as redistributive effects on employment and output.[13]

x. The Costs and Consequences of Inflation

It might be imagined in the first instance that inflation, whilst a symptom of crisis, has no harmful effects as such. That transactions take place at increasing prices is of no matter as long as the real transactions do take place. Indeed, when taking account of inflationary expectations, it has been seen that real economic activity can be stimulated by the flight from money. When it is a choice between inflation and unemployment surely the former should prevail?

However we have already seen that once inflation becomes anticipated, it can be argued that it can accelerate even with declining levels of employment. Unless no weight is to be given to the objective of inflation then it has to be controlled within fairly narrow limits (for otherwise not at all), and there are reasons to control inflation since immediately and ultimately it affects the workings of the real economy.

First, an accelerating inflation generates social and economic instability. Even if inflation is fully anticipated, economic contracting will be increasingly undertaken outside the efficient allocative mechanism of market supply and demand. At the very least, barter begins to replace the efficient mediation of exchange by money. Where inflation is incorrectly anticipated, there are redistributive effects, and particular income recipients suffer (i.e. those on fixed money incomes). Monetarists also tend to argue that increases in the money supply to finance state expenditure and the subsequent inflation are a means by which all disposable incomes are reduced as the state struggles to find the most politically acceptable means of increasing taxation. This can generate economic and social conflict, as well as obstructing the adjustment of relative marginal productivities to appropriate relative prices. The movement of absolute prices may be so rapid that it dominates the reallocative movement of relative prices.

Second, as we have seen, inflation reduces real balances held as a result of a flight from depreciating money. This has the welfare cost of decreasing the utility gained from holding real balances. Nor is this some illusory lust for the glister of gold. Individuals must make more frequent trips to the bank and bear greater precautionary risks. For banks, the results are analogous but more devastating. Their reserve ratio will be reduced as greater risk is borne in the face of the higher cost of holding money. Consequently bank failures are more likely, so that all in all the financial system as a whole is subject to greater instability.

Third, even when inflation is fully anticipated in aggregate terms, all prices will not increase continuously in proportion to each other. Consequently, knowledge of relative prices (including wages) will be more uncertain than when prices are simply changing for reallocative purposes alone. A reduction in knowledge can itself be considered an economic cost with effects on the real economy. For example, it can be argued that more time will be spent searching out the best wage rate when workers change jobs so that the structural level of unemployment is increased.

xi. International Aspects of Inflation

It is not the intention of this chapter to survey international economics as well as the economics of inflation. But, if we are to relate theories of inflation to the current world economy then it is not possible to be silent on international aspects of inflation. Fortunately, the bourgeois theories of inflation in an international context are more or less identical to the propositions developed for the closed economy. The pretentious claim to deal with the world economy depends upon a feint of hand that substitutes categories of international economics for those of the closed economy.[14]

Essentially this is done by replacing individuals and/or groups in the closed economy by nations. The overall framework of Keynesianism remains unimpaired, although the relative significance of cost-push/demand — pull and price/quantity adjustment remains a matter for controversy (and estimation). The interests of the nation are represented by as large an expansion of domestic output as possible, *ceteris paribus*, but the instruments for achieving this domestically (fiscal and monetary policy related to the money supply, interest rate, taxes and budget deficit) may lead to international imbalance (balance of payments disequilibrium or exchange rate movement) or frustration as international monetary flows counteract domestic monetary policy.

All will be well as long as the overall level of demand in the world economy does not correspond to a level of employment above the natural rate. Otherwise, self-fulfilling expectations about inflations or movements in other variables (such as exchange rates) will be transmitted internationally and generate domestically the effects already analysed for the closed economy. Differences may exist over the appropriate international and domestic policies to be adopted to restore equilibrium according to the variety of Keynesianism utilized. Cost-push influences become transformed into conflicts between nations over distributive shares of output and employment and can be measured against indices of power and changes in power in the world economy.

xii. Inflation and the Current Crisis

Our consideration of bourgeois inflation theory leads us to understand that the current world economy will be analysed and prescribed for on the basis of a number of fundamental propositions. First, there is an equilibrium (including a natural level of unemployment) which it is the object of policy to attain with minimum adjustment cost. Second, essential to this objective is the reduction of the rate of inflation so that the vicious spiral of self-fulfilling inflationary expectations is broken. Third, this can only be done by short-run policies that reduce the level of employment below the natural rate, so that inflation and expectations of it are reduced in the short-run, and subsequently abolished in the long-run, by deflationary policies. Fourth, this aggregate solution for the world economy must be distributed throughout the individual economies according to a combination of international political and economic settlements. Fifth, the individual national levels of deflation must be accepted within those nations. Sixth, in so far as these policies are not adopted and accepted at all of the international and national levels necessary, stagflation will persist and, if reflationary policies are renewed too early, return. Seventh, the movement of the world economy away from its initial path of equilibrium growth — the post-war boom — has to be explained by some disturbance stimulating inflationary expectations.

On the first six of these propositions, we need make little more comment. They will be familiar to every reader in one form or another in the context of economic policy in their own country.[15] Different theorists and policy-makers give different emphases to different policies, but the outcome is always the same. [16] As suggested by the third proposition, real wage cuts, social service cuts and increases in unemployment, whether rationalized and implemented through incomes policy and or cuts in the budget deficit, growth in the money supply or government expenditure are all necessary to reduce the level of (expected) inflation in the short-run and restore equilibrium in the long-run. In addition, the economic theory that informs these policy suggestions is open to a presentation for popular ideology, that over-expansion of the money supply, state expenditure or wages causes inflation.

Explanations in response to the seventh proposition are open to more variability. Most popular is the reliance upon one or more 'exogenous' development in or shock to the economic system. For example, the rise in prices of primary commodities through natural depletion or the flexing of the economic muscles of newly independent colonies (in particular the OPEC countries) is seen as a stimulus to inflation in the developed economies. It can also be seen to lead to distributional conflict between the advanced and third-world countries, as well as posing the problem of financial recycling the revenues involved. An alternative explanation relies upon the growth of trade union power, monopolization and increasing state economic intervention in the attempt to maintain political power. Yet again, it can be argued that American domination of the world economy has been challenged so that dollars are no longer accepted as a world money supply, releasing resources for American use in Vietnam or elsewhere. Characteristic of these explanations is that they concern forces that are accidental, temporary and, where economic conflicts and scapegoats are involved, open to satisfactory solution. Equilibrium can be restored given political agreement *and* temporary sacrifice.

xiii. Forms of Credit[17]

It will perhaps have occurred to the reader that whilst both of the theories presented bear upon the causes of the current world recession, neither has any point of contact with the other. The bourgeois theory fails to deal with the accumulation and restructuring of international capital, the class antagonisms to which these give rise and the relationship between these and the role of the state in economic and social reproduction. The organizing concept for the theory is the existence of an equilibrium and associated with it a level of frictional unemployment that is necessary for the smooth functioning of allocation through the market system. Clearly this equilibrium level of necessary, even 'desirable', unemployment is a pale reflection of the cyclical rhythm of unemployment associated with the accumulation of capital. Nevertheless, variations in the level of unemployment are explained in terms of the aggregate response of individuals to expected rates of inflation. The higher is the expected rate of inflation, the higher is the level of unemployment associated with a given level of actual inflation. Because of the post war boom, it is presumed that the world economy has been more or less in non-inflationary equilibrium prior to an exogenous (or arbitrarily explained) disturbance that has led automatically to an inflationary and unemployment disequilibrium, or even stagflationary equilibrium the cure for which is the short and sharp sacrifice of deflationary policies.

On the other hand, the analysis offered in the first section does not confront the problem of explaining inflation, even if it does examine the forces promoting the post-war expansion and the limitations upon them. Nor, however, is an explanation of inflation precluded by the analysis, in the same way that the bourgeois theory's preoccupation with equilibrium precludes an understanding of the contradictory development of capital accumulation. Nevertheless, the concepts for analysing inflation cannot simply be borrowed from the bourgeois theory for otherwise the explanation of inflation will be rooted within bourgeois theory. For example, radical theories of inflation often emphasize class struggle as its cause in either one of two ways. Distributional struggle over wages forces up costs and consequently prices, further intensifying the conflict over the shares of available national income. Alternatively, it is often argued that class struggle forces the state to borrow and expand the money supply, in order to finance social services or maintain the level of employment, consequently fuelling inflation. Theoretically, these two theories correspond to the orthodox explanations of cost-push and demand-pull inflation, even if the irreconcilable differences between classes are seen as the systematic source of disequilibrium rather than the intervention of expectations into the harmonious workings of the market.[18]

In order to construct an alternative theory of inflation, and one based on the accumulation of capital, we have to examine the concepts of credit and money critically. Orthodox theory, for example, rooted in Keynesianism tends to see credit as an undifferentiated concept, the expansion of which, say in the form of an increased money supply, simply adds to aggregate demand and consequently inflation in the face of the failure to expand output. Credit, however, can be extended for two rather different reasons. First, there is the motive associated with the ability to make exchanges. The time of sale and purchase is separated from the time of payment with either transactor making a temporary loan to the other according to whether payment is made in advance or in arrears of the exchange itself.

Second, however, credit is extended for the purpose of making a profit or more accurately to gain interest. It follows conversely that the borrower must have the intention of using the loan to contribute to making a profit for otherwise the interest could not be paid (together presumably with something left over). Now in orthodox theory, both of these forms of credit are synonymous, the first reflecting intertemporal preferences over consumption (interest being paid for a delay or advance of payment possibly in the form of a higher or lower price respectively — credit or cash terms) and the second reflecting intertemporal production possibilities.

However, from our analysis of section one, we have seen that credit of the second type, normally in money-form, is of considerable importance for the accumulation of capital. For the use of money as capital is the means by which financial restructuring takes place and is a means by which individual capitals seek to survive and compete during that restructuring by controlling and utilizing as large a mass of capital as possible. It follows that the expansion of this form of the credit system is a necessary secular development for capitalism (although cyclical reductions in the credit system are also a feature of crises of recessions).

On the other hand, credit of the first type even where it involves interest payments, does not belong to an analysis of the competition between capitals to expand productivity during the accumulation process. It merely involves a redistribution of the times (and also the sizes) of payments by consumers. Consider this in the context of the way in which wages are paid. Workers do receive and have received credit in many different forms. These range from the factory shops and pawnshops of nineteenth-century capitalism through to the hire purchase and mortgage arrangements of the present day. Even where these forms of credit have not had the effect of simply reducing the value of real wages, they have always had the effect of adding coercion to the wage-labourer to work in order to maintain the levels of physical consumption, comforts and housing as the case may be. The same holds true for the instances where the worker makes savings and receives interest payments. For, in general, far from this reflecting the freedom of the worker to spread earnings over a lifetime of consumption, it reflects the means by which the worker is forced to work when able to do so in order to provide for the times when unable to do so (or to earn the deposits necessary for a house, car, etc). The force of these remarks is to demonstrate that the role played by credit is to be located at two different levels of analysis, one to be associated with the competitive accumulation between capitalists, the other with the distributional struggle between capital and labour over the form in which wage goods are provided as well as the quantities provided.

In addition, the same sort of distinctions must be applied to state expenditure, the creation of a budget deficit and the state's interventions into the credit system (whether to expand the money supply or not). For these do not correspond to some amorphous set of undifferentiated payments or loans as in Keynesian analysis of aggregate demand. In contrast, the state's expenditure, for example, is in part made as capital — when funding investment in nationalized industries and aid to private capital — and presupposes an expansion of profitable production, and in part it functions purely as a means of allocating surplus already produced — when financing military expenditure or welfare services, for example-without presupposing a further expansion of output. Of course, it could be argued, and this is the basis for all bourgeois inflation theory, that if the credit had not been expanded and/or if the expenditure had not been made, and/or if output had expanded, there could be no inflation. But we can see that such arguments have no specific roots in an analysis of the capitalist economy, for which expenditures as capital specifically require an expansion of output whereas other expenditures do not, but draw upon existing resources.

Now reconsider the credit given in the processes of buying and selling. Again, this can be seen to have the effect of simply easing the process of exchange. But, where credit is granted, it does tend to affect the size of payment, in strict correspondence to the time of credit and rate of interest. In addition, a class of merchant capitalists and banking capitalists can intercede between the buyers and sellers to improve the efficiency and make a profit on the business of arranging exchanges and loans. The result is that the first form of credit we have considered, that related to buying and selling, becomes subordinated to specific forms of capital specializing in these functions and making a profit from them. In other words, as capitalism develops, all credit tends to become linked to the existence of credit as capital, although it does not all become directed towards expansion of capital in the process of production but can also be used for commercial and financial purposes.

This is confirmed if we reconsider the credit relationship between capital and labour. In the place of the credit between the worker and his employer's shop which represents more or less directly a struggle over the level of wages, we find the credit between capital and labour mediated socially by the intervention of capital through bank loans, hire-purchase agreements and building societies. Similar conclusions hold if we consider state expansion of credit. Whether brought about through an expansion of the money supply or by borrowing, this usually involves a direct interaction with private financial institutions (or nationalized industries) geared to the making of profit on the basis of those credit operations. On the other hand, the state can appear at times to expand the money supply purely to make income 'transfers', for example, to increase old-age pensions. On accounting grounds, it is wrong to identify the expansion of the money supply with one object of expenditure rather than another (just as it is wrong to argue that a government deficit is caused by one set of expenditures rather than others). All we can say is that overall the level of the money supply has been increased. The problem is whether this constitutes an overall expansion of money as means of payment or more specifically as capital.

It could be argued that since pensioners in general are not capitalists, no expansion of money as capital is involved. This would be wrong unless pensioners confined their expenditures between themselves and other non-capitalist agents. But this is scarcely the case. Rather, money-capital will have been expanded indirectly through the intermediary of the pensioners concerned. For the income 'transfer' immediately passes into the hands of capitalists (who sell the commodities to pensioners) and they can utilize as capital the money obtained. This of course differs from a straight expansion of the money supply to subsidize the capitalists concerned since it also involves *ceteris paribus* a distribution of surplus to pensioners. But these two effects are to be separated conceptually and that this is so is demonstrated by the fact that the state could have made that distribution through fiscal policy alone. It follows that the use to which the money expansion has been put corresponds both to a redistribution of surplus and a general expansion of money-capital. That the two effects have been accomplished simultaneously (and even this is not true) should not mislead us into believing that the expansion of the money supply has not been one of capital.

This has been a long and difficult section because it confronts the problem of the role of credit in such a way as to produce at times counter-intuitive arguments not only to those trained in Keynesian categories of analysis but also to popular common-sense. We have not dealt with every possible case of the nature of the credit relations between state, capital and labour, but the following general conclusions can be drawn. First, credit as a means simply of easing buying and selling must be distinguished from credit that is advanced as capital and which is necessarily linked to an expansion of output and payment of interest. Orthodox theory fails to make this distinction by aggregating together all factors contributing to effective demand (although it does determine the rate of interest by reference to the supply of and demand for money). Second, then, orthodox theory emphasizes the role played by money as a means of payment in the formation of the level of effective demand. In contrast, it can be argued that it is the role played by money as capital that predominates even when money is expanded through the state purely for the purpose of making purchases possible in the first instance (for income transfers or military expenditure, for example). In addition, it can be observed that the development of the subordination of credit as means of payment to credit as capital stimulates the operations of financial and commercial as well as of industrial capital.

The paradoxical nature of these results cannot be overemphasized. At a time when the simple expansion of credit seems greater than ever before as loans are made to workers in various forms, as workers save and as the state expands the money supply to finance social services, it is being argued that credit is increasingly being expanded as capital! The paradox is resolved by not looking at these developments from the perspective of an individual, whether capitalist, labourer or Treasury official, but by examining the *capitalist* system *as a whole*. For then, these credit relations can be seen to be veils drawn over the form in which wages are paid and social services distributed[19] as opposed to the process of competition between capitalists to promote financial restructuring.

xiv. Credit as Capital and Inflation

It is now our intention to draw the relationship between the role of credit as capital and the process of inflation. First, it should be observed that the fact that credit acts as capital neither implies logically that there should be price deflation, inflation nor stability. It depends upon the extent to which credit as capital is advanced successfully in terms of generating productivity increase and consequently extra surplus out of which interest can be paid. Consequently, in order to determine the rate of inflation we have to examine the forces behind a successful expansion of capital as well as those behind the expansion of credit as capital.

To a great extent we have already accomplished this task in Section 1. There we saw that accumulation necessarily assumed a cyclical pattern as the process of restructuring capital is punctuated by crises and recessions. The expansion of credit as capital tends to follow that same cyclical rhythm, as individual capitalists compete for credit to establish large-scale units of production with higher and higher levels of productivity. But as this process of competitive accumulation draws to a close credit as capital will have been over-expanded and lead to inflation. This follows from the fact that productivity increase and surplus production will not correspond to the levels presupposed by the advance of credit as capital. Nevertheless, it will appear as if there is too much credit relative to production and this gives rise to orthodox theory's preoccupation with aggregate demand as opposed to the role played by credit as capital in the accumulation process. Further, once begun this inflationary process will tend to fuel speculation (for example, precisely in those commodity markets with increasing prices). Eventually, a crash in some branch of exchange or speculation will break, and the economy will be plunged into recession (the effects of which we discuss below as far as price movements are concerned).

Now, a natural question is why the expansion of credit as capital had to exceed the expansion of capital in production and why could it not have been restricted to non-inflationary levels even in the movement into recession. Even leaving aside the role played by speculation, such a question reveals a Keynesian understanding of the role played by credit, that the level of aggregate demand simply needs to correspond to the level of output. In contrast, we have argued that competitive accumulation requires the expansion of credit as capital to bring about the reorganization and expansion of production but it does not thereby determine the level of output (and surplus) produced, for that depends upon the strength and forms of class resistance to accumulation. If the credit expansion had been restricted, the effect would have been to precipitate the elimination of a number of capitals, and possibly a recession, as these would be unable to expand and so remain competitive. To suggest that credit expansion can at all times correspond to output expansion is to ignore the necessity of the cycle of production and the role played in it by competitive accumulation. It would be like suggesting that two teams after struggling to a five-all draw would have been better off to have settled for nil-nil at the outset!

So much for the tendency to inflation towards the end of the boom and its speculative sequel. In the following recession, there is a tendency towards a depreciation in prices (and appreciation of money). The reason for this is that with the crash in the credit system and the movement into recession, there is an excess of capital in all its forms — in production, commodities and paper claims to dividends and interest. These all lose their exchange value relative to money, to one degree or another according to the process of competition between the capitalists concerned. Although there has been an over-expansion of money-capital as well as other forms of capital, the former tends to appreciate relative to the latter since it is the universally accepted means of payment and most advantageous means of hoarding idle capital. This means idle machinery and workers, a collapse in the values of paper assets and a *fall* in the level of prices. This would appear to leave inexplicable the coexistence of increasing unemployment and inflation, the development over which bourgeois theory only stumbles by appending a theory of expectations. But as yet we have not examined the role played by the state in the credit system and its relationship to inflation.

xv. The State and Inflation

Earlier we have examined the increasing economic intervention by the state and in particular its role in relation to the credit system. The role of the state in expanding credit must be distinguished from the private expansion of credit for two related reasons. First, it is not geared to individual private profit-making (although it does in general operate to promote the profitable expansion of production), and this allows the state to moderate the rhythm of the cycle of production and possibly to moderate its effects through its control of the level of credit in general. Second, the expansion of state credit may take the form of the expansion of the money supply.

Taken together, these two conditions mean that just as the state does not seek to make a profit out of its interventions into the credit system, so also it does not run the risk of its financial assets becoming bankrupted. Contrast the situation with the private credit system. There, for example, the collapse following a speculative boom leads to an uneven depreciation of the financial assets concerned as some become worthless and as others lose more or less value. For the state, the financial asset concerned predominantly in the formation of credit is money. The spread of losses over it must be even since it is a single and homogeneous asset. Consequently, the over-expansion of credit as capital through the state becomes an over-expansion of money and leads to a uniform depreciation of money, i.e. inflation, rather than an uneven depreciation of a mixed set of assets and credit relations. This is an effect furthered by another process associated with the development of state credit, the displacement of a commodity money such as gold, not by paper money as a substitute, but altogether. As a result, during a recession, the flight to money as such and away from other forms of capital is less pronounced (although it does lead to more pronounced movements between one form of international currency and another with well known results.)

From these observations it follows that the rhythm of price increases does not follow the cycle of production as in the case of the private credit system. Rather inflation may accelerate during the recession even above the levels achieved during the previous speculative boom. Does this mean that inflation is simply explained by an over-expansion of state credit, particularly in the form of money? If so, the Keynesian (and in particular the modern monetarist) theory would appear to have been restored with a vengeance and much needless rhetoric.

To demonstrate that this is not so the distinctive features of the theory of inflation constructed will be brought out. First, enough has been said about the differences in the concepts of credit (and money) involved that they do not bear repeating. Second, however, these different analyses of the credit system are not accidental but naturally belong respectively to the Keynesian or Marxist analyses of the economy for which they are constructed and with which they are integrated. Thus, the Keynesian theory of credit can no more belong to a theory of the accumulation and centralization of capital, than the Marxist theory of credit (and its two forms) can have any relevance for Keynesian theory.

Third then, this becomes specifically clear when it is observed that all bourgeois theory is organized around the concept of equilibrium. It is usually presumed that this equilibrium (and its associated levels of employment and natural unemployment) can eventually be maintained with price stability through an expansion of the money supply proportionate to the rate of increase of productivity. In contrast, we have argued that there is no such equilibrium and that these movements in the credit system cannot be taken to be exogenous nor be explained by an appended sociological theory of the motivation of governments to retain political power. Rather it is argued that there are systematic forces leading to an over-expansion of the credit system relative to the pace of competitive accumulation, and that this can give rise to stagflation, as opposed to deflation, the more the state intervenes in the credit system, as it must do, with the development of state monopoly capitalism.

Further Reading

During the preparation of this chapter, I benefitted by consulting the surveys of Frisch (1977) and Laidler and Parkin (1975) to remind me of the orthodox approaches to inflation theory. The reader might prefer to consult a standard text book such as Trevithick and Mulvey (1975). Those interested in radical theories of inflation might like to begin with Harvey (1977). A selection of writings by orthodox economists on the problems of and solutions to the current world recession is to be found in 'Crisis '75. . .?', Institute of Economic Affairs, Occasional Paper 43, 1975.

Frisch, M. (1977), 'Inflation Theory 1963-1975: A "Second Generation" Survey', *Journal of Economic Literature*, December 1977, vol. XV, no. 4.

Harvey, J. (1977), 'Inflation Theory' *Marxism Today*, January 1977.

Laidler, D. and M. Parkin (1975), 'Inflation: A Survey', *Economic Journal*, December 1975, 85 (340).

Trevithick J. and C. Mulvey (1975), *The Economics of Inflation*, Martin Robertson, London.

The following articles referred to in the footnotes are to be found in F. Green and P. Nore, *Issues in Political Economy*, MacMillan, 1979, in which this chapter also first appeared:

S. Himmelweit, 'Accumulation and Reproduction of Economic Systems'.

J. Grahl, 'A Critique of Econometrics'.

F. Green, 'The Consumption Function and Neo-Classical Theories of Saving: A Critique'.

L. Harris, 'The Role of Money in the Economy'.

Notes to Chapter 4

1. Consideration of economic and social reproduction is to be found at greater length in Himmelweit (1979).
2. The quantity theory is considered at greater length in Harris (1979).
3. In addition, the rate of interest will have fallen stimulating the investment that increases employment and output. We have not dealt here with the cases of the vertical IS curve and horizontal LM curve for which employment cannot be raised, but neither of these necessarily lead to inflation.
4. This explanation is usually made by reference to the Keynesian 'cross'.
5. Alternatively, it could be argued that individuals suffer from money illusion.
6. The price of bonds yielding a steady income of one per annum can be shown to be worth l/r, that is to be inversely related to the rate of interest.

7. It is not necessary for there to be full employment in every sector of the economy, but it is necessary for full employment to be obtained in an essential (for example, skilled) sector of the labour force, giving rise to a 'bottleneck' to the expansion of output. Alternatively, there could be a bottleneck for some scarce resource, such as a primary commodity.
8. An extended treatment of controversies in macro-economic policy, cannot be undertaken here. It can be observed here however, that there are so many potential variations in the structure and specification of the Keynesian model, that any empirical development of macro-economic aggregates can be accommodated by a whole series of conflicting models. Each model has sufficient variation in the values of parameters, the variables to be included and the structure and lags in the model to 'explain' (if not predict) empirical economic developments. See Grahl (1979) for a criticism of macro-econometric models. Also, see Green (1979), where it can be seen that the theory of the consumption function affects the size of adjustments. Indeed, monetarists can argue that unless individuals suffer from 'tax illusion', an increase in government expenditure can at best be marginally inflationary at full employment if it is not financed by an increase in the money supply, since anticipated tax increases in the future will reduce desired present consumption.
9. It is necessary to observe that it is possible for real and money wages to increase at the same rate as productivity increase without price inflation.
10. Thus, the growth of the money supply is a sufficient condition for the maintenance of and even acceleration of inflation, but is it a necessary condition? Logically, it is possible for inflation to accelerate without an increase in the money supply, if the reactions to expected inflation are particularly extreme. Real money balances may be run down to purchase real goods at such a rapid rate that inflation is funded by this alone.
11. It is also possible to hypothesize a leading sector within a group, as for wage bargaining for example.
12. However, it can be argued within the cost-push framework that the government acts in the interests of capital. See below.
13. The analysis of this properly belongs elsewhere as it can be understood in macro-economics in isolation from the process of inflation.
14. There is a clear analogy here with bourgeois theory of international trade, which is treated more or less as a world economy of trading individuals (as nations).
15. It should be observed however that many governments present their economic problems as unique as an ideological justification for failure relative to other economies and for stringent economic policies to restore success.
16. For example, monetarists emphasize deflationary policies through limitation in the growth of the money supply, trade unionists tend to support wage and price restraint in return for the *promise* of a commitment to policies stimulating growth and employment.
17. See also Harris (1979).
18. Radical theories also often see inflation as a state conspiracy to tax wages as do monetarists!
19. It is not being suggested that these 'veils' have no effect as in bourgeois theories of the real economy and neutrality of money (e.g., the pre-Keynesian quantity theory). In particular, they concern both the forms taken by class struggle over the level of wages and social services as well as intra-class conflict among the commercial, banking and industrial fractions of the bourgeoisie.

5

Diversions in the Theory of Capital

i. The Propositions of Neo-Classical Capital Theory

As the Cambridge capital controversy or critique takes as its subject for debate the validity or usefulness of the one-sector model associated with neo-classical growth theory, it is as well to begin with an exposition of that model. It has as its central concept an aggregate production function which relates the level of output Y to the levels of inputs used. These inputs comprise capital K and labour L, where K comprises the same physical good as Y, truly a one-good world. In mathematical terms, $Y = F(K, L)$ where F is the production function. The higher is K or L, correspondingly the higher will be the level of output. Intuitively, the rationale behind the construction of the aggregate production function is the idea of an individual production process where the use of more inputs will lead to an increase in output. Its application, however, is to the inputs and outputs for the economy as a whole. As a result, a multitude of difficulties are concealed in the measurement of outputs and inputs by single indices, particularly as the relative as well as the absolute proportions of the input and outputs concerned may vary. It is these difficulties that lie at the bottom of the critique of the neo-classical model. But we anticipate subsequent sections. Before moving on, it is nevertheless worthwhile digressing to comment on the social content implicit in the conceptualization of production as a mathematical function. It presumes that the labour process is a fixed technical relation (for example, like the formation of water — H_2O), involving the harmonious and symmetrical interaction of capital and labour to form output.

Carrying on regardless, the neo-classical model begins to restrict the functions F that may be permitted to stand as representatives of production possibilities in aggregate. We have already demanded that F be an increasing function of both K and L, we also require that F exhibit constant returns to scale, that a proportionate increase in both the inputs leads to an expansion of output in the same proportion. Whatever the plausibility of this assumption for an individual production process, let alone for the economy as a whole, (the existence of social goods must be denied or are we to duplicate parliament and the telephone system, etc?), it certainly generates a certain analytical convenience, in the light of which the perceptive cynic might observe that the mathematics rules the economics rather than vice-versa (more generally it might be suspected that the necessary conditions to generate a competitive equilibrium come to dominate neo-classical theorizing rather than a concerted effort to be 'realistic', however correctly or not being realistic is itself theorized). Once the production function is taken to satisfy the conditions for constant returns to scale, then two things follow. First, a proportionate increase in one factor alone, say K, must lead to a less than proportionate increase in output. For to obtain a proportionate increase in output the other input L must have been increased in the same proportion as K. But, as it has not, output must have increased less than in proportion to the single input. In other words, the more an input increases, then the progressively smaller is the associated increase in output. Neo-classical economics expresses this in its terminology as a diminishing marginal product to each input.

The second property of the constant returns to scale economy is that it can be represented in per capita terms. All economies with the same capital per man (or more exactly employee) will have the same output per man (given the same underlying production function), although the absolute level of output will depend upon the absolute amount of capital (and numbers of workers). Each economy will be an enlargement or reduction of each other that has the same ratio of capital to labour. If we denote K/L by k and Y/L by y, then the production function can be rewritten in per capita terms as $y=f(k)$.

Now, the earlier property of diminishing marginal product of capital is simply carried over to the per capita representation of production possibilities. An increase in capital per man will lead to an increase in output per man but less than in proportion. If, in addition, it is presumed that with zero capital, the level of output must also be zero, then the relationship between output per man and capital per man is as represented in diagram 5.1.

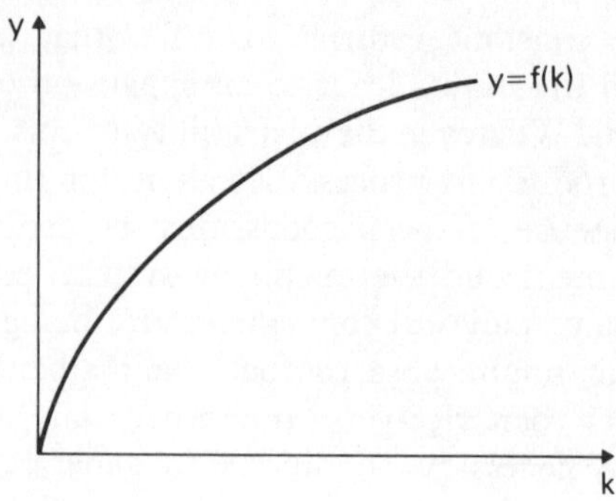

Diagram 5.1

So much for the neo-classical model's specification of the conditions of production. It leads, however, to a theory of distribution based on perfect competition. For suppose that the rate of interest (or rate of profit — the two are interchangeably used in this moneyless economy) is denoted by r, then r represents the 'price of capital'. Of course, r is the price that would have to be paid for borrowing the use of capital for a unit period of time. For perfect competition, every economic agent takes r as given. Profit maximization per man implies maximizing f(k)-rk-w where w is the wage per man. Mathematically, this yields $f'(k)=r$ or equivalently, in the neo-classical terminology, it can easily be intuitively argued that the marginal product of capital MPC must be equal to the rate of interest. From the conditions of profit maximization, the wage rate can also be deduced as the marginal product of labour MPL yielding a slightly more complicated expression, namely, $w=f(k)-kf'(k)$. It necessarily follows (and this derives from the original assumption of constant returns) that the sum of profit per man and wage per man just exhausts the net output produced $y = rk + w$.

The mathematics of these results need not concern us unduly. They are in any case open to convenient graphical representation and further analysis. Because the rate of profit equals the marginal product of capital, it equals the slope of the production function at the appropriate value of k (see diagram 5.2).

It now follows from the shape of the production function (which in turn is dependent upon the assumption of diminishing marginal products) that the rate of profit declines as capital per man

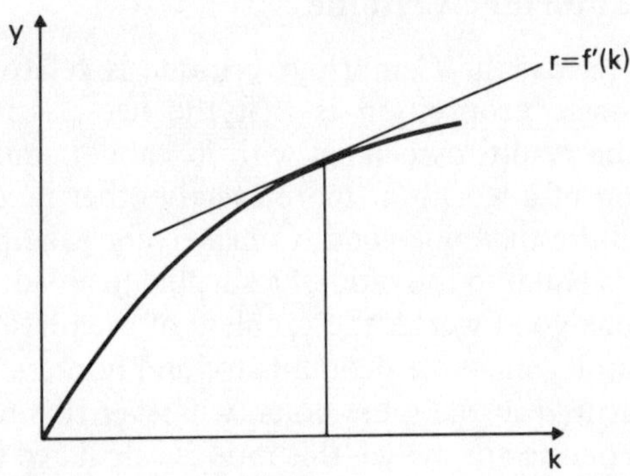

Diagram 5.2

increases, as represented in diagram 5.3, since the slope of the production function declines as k increases.

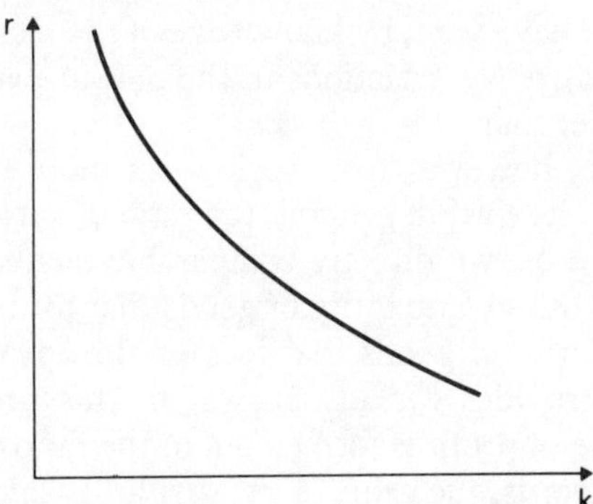

Diagram 5.3

Moving on now from these technical derivations it is necessary to bring out their significance as economic propositions. Quite apart from the implied direction of the relationships between the various variables, the outstanding result of the analysis is that distribution is determined by technological relations alone. To be more precise the values of r and w can be calculated once the production possibilities as a whole, namely f, and the particular endowment of resources in use, yielding k, are known. For then, quite simply, $r = f'(k)$ (and $w = f(k) - kf'(k)$). It is this proposition, that technology alone determines distribution that is special to the neo-classical one sector model and which forms the basis for what appears to be a devastating critique.

ii. The Cambridge Critique

In informal terms, the Cambridge critique is relatively simple to follow. Its basic proposition is that the neo-classical one-sector model and the results associated with it, cannot stand as a simple representation of a world (or more exactly other models) in which there exists more than one good. Consider, for example, the rate of profit. This is equal to the ratio of a surplus to an advance. Now, if we are in a one-good world, the problem of calculating this ratio is relatively simple, since the denominator and numerator of the fraction are measured in the same units, whatever this may be. In the neo-classical one-sector model, this ratio is calculated on the basis of perfect competition to be the marginal product of capital, the marginal increment of output for a marginal increment of capital or $\frac{\Delta y}{\Delta k}$ as Δk tends to zero. Consequently, the rate of profit can be determined as we have seen, by knowledge of the technical relations of production that relate variations in the output per man to variations in capital per man.

Once we move, however, to a world with more than one good, then problems arise. For, in general, the ratio of surplus to advance will not be a ratio of two directly comparable quantities. How is a ratio to be found out of a quantity of goods that form the surplus in relation to a quantity of goods that formed the advance of capital? In fact, reality provides a ready answer to this problem. We all know that the rate of profit is formed out of the ratio of two (money) values. In other words, the value of the surplus is calculated relative to the value of the advance at current prices. But such a calculation remains a mere tautology, it cannot be said to form a theory of the determination of the rate of profit, and more generally distribution. For, in order to work out the rate of profit, we need to know prices, and to know prices, we need to know the rate of profit, because, for example, more capital-intensive products will have higher prices, the higher is the rate of interest. The derivation of the rate of profit from a ratio of surplus to advance (which is a way of seeking the marginal product of capital) is then purely circular.

The problem outlined in the previous paragraph has often been described as the problem of aggregating capital. When a production function is used, what are the units in which K is to be measured? To some extent, the problem of aggregating capital is a misnomer.

To be pedantic capital can be easily aggregated in all sorts of ways, by weight, volume or even current prices. More seriously, the problem is to aggregate capital in such a way that the propositions of neo-classical theory remain valid — that a production function can be formed from which marginal products yield distribution. As such, this is not necessarily a problem of aggregating different sorts of capital goods, since the problem still arises even if there is only one capital good (as long as there is also a different consumption good). Rather, it is the problem of evaluating or indexing capital so that the rate of profit can be not only formed but determined by technological relations. What the Cambridge critique does is to show that the problem cannot be solved, and we proceed now to demonstrate this more formally.

Consider an economy in which there are two goods, say corn and machines, one is solely used for consumption, the other for production — both of itself and of corn. In addition, labour is used as an input in the two production processes. In effect, corn is produced by a *technique* which first involves the production of machines by labour alone and then involves the production of corn by machinery and labour. (Obviously, this is not a very realistic example since corn is required besides machinery, for its own production but that is by the way). A technique then consists of the two production processes. Let us suppose that to produce corn a quantity of machinery a and ℓ of labour is required and the quantities to produce machinery are b and n respectively. Now let p be the price of machinery and w the wage rate in terms of corn as numeraire, with r the rate of profit on capital advanced. Now, if competition ensures that p,w and r are equalized across the economy, then the following equations hold, assuming that wages are paid after production is completed.

$$pa(1+r)+w\ell = 1$$
$$pb(1+r)+wn = p$$

These equations simply reflect that costs plus profit must equal prices for each of the production processes. Now, from these two equations in the three unknowns p,w, and r, p can be eliminated to leave an equation relating r and w. This is $r = \dfrac{1-w\ell}{b+w(na-\ell b)} - 1$

Although this equation is quite complicated it has properties which can be represented quite simply graphically. (The interested reader can, if so inclined, verify the correspondence between the graphical properties and the equations by means of calculus). The possible relationships between w and r are illustrated in diagram 5.4. The graphs are called factor price frontiers for the techniques concerned. In each case, w and r are inversely related, an increase in the wage rate must lead to a fall in the rate of profit. Otherwise, the factor price frontier is bent outwards, a straight line, or bent inwards according to whether $\frac{a}{\ell}$ is less than, equal to or greater than $\frac{b}{n}$. In technical terms, the ratios $\frac{a}{\ell}$ and $\frac{b}{n}$ measure the capital (i.e. machine) intensity of production of corn and machines, respectively, relative to the labour employed. The shape of the factor price frontier (fpf for short) for the technique is determined by the relative factor-input intensities.

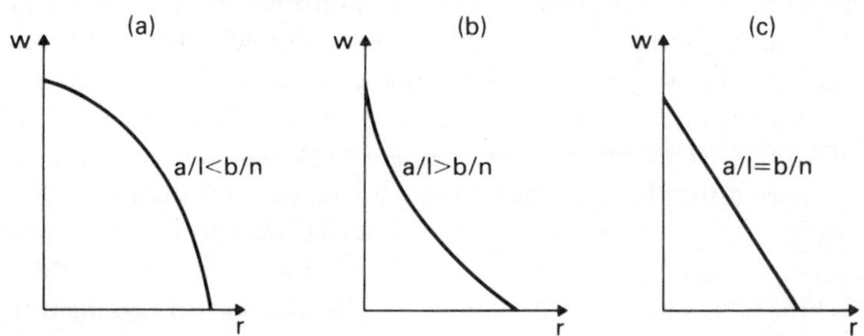

Diagram 5.4

Before proceeding further, it is necessary to make two assumptions that have the effect of simplifying the exposition, but which it can be stated are not necessary to produce the results that will be obtained. First, as already indicated, it will be presumed that there is one good used solely for consumption, and another used solely as capital. Second, it will be assumed that the economy is in a stationary state, that there is no growth. These two assumptions taken together have the effect of reducing the problem at hand to the very minimum. For they mean that net output consists solely of the single consumption good (no growth implies no net output of machines) and the advance is made solely as a single capital good. Thus, the formation of the rate of profit as the ratio of a surplus and an advance becomes relatively simple to analyse.

The restriction of the economy to two goods has the effect, however, of limiting the shapes that can be taken by the technique fpf according to those illustrated in diagram 5.4. If more goods were permitted then the possible fpf's would admit more shapes. They would remain downward sloping, but could have wiggles in them as illustrated in diagram 5.5. (Again, the reader with sufficiently developed calculus will be able to demonstrate this. It can be shown that the number of possible wiggles is one less than the number of capital goods). Accordingly, we will use a wiggly technique fpf where necessary, although this will always be to simplify graphical exposition rather than because of strict mathematical requirements for more than one capital good.

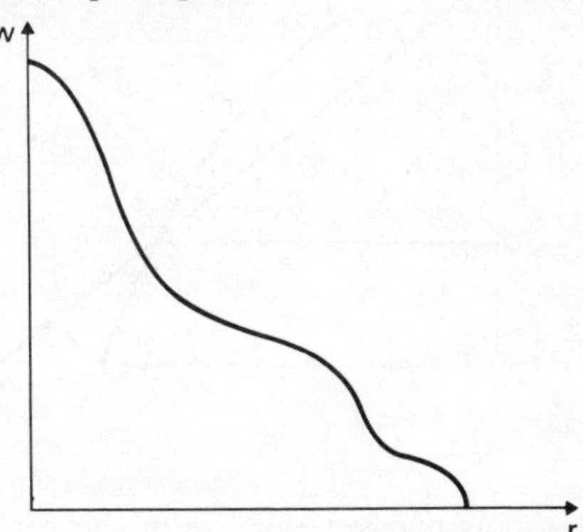

Diagram 5.5

Now for the use of this technique, there will be generated a certain amount of output per man y which is in fact, a quantity of corn for consumption. It will be divided between wages per man w and profits. These profits will equal rk where r is the rate of profit and k is the *value* of capital used in the economy. Thus, k is not simply the quantity of physical capital used, the number of machines determined by a multiplied by the output of corn added to b multiplied by the output of machines. Rather, k is this quantity of machines, multiplied by their price p, to give as stated the value of capital. The relationship between y,k,r, and w can be expressed in terms of a sort of national income accounts per man.

$$y = kr + w$$

From this equation, it follows that $k = \frac{y-w}{r}$ as a simple reformulation of national income accounting. In other words, if we know y,w, and r then we can determine k. How this is done graphically is represented in diagram 5.6, from which it will be demonstrated that k equals tan A, or for those unfamiliar with trigonometry, the slope of the line CBA (leaving aside its negative sign). This line joins the intercept of the fpf on the w-axis C to the point of distribution B, where w and r take on particular values for the technique. The extension of the line CB cuts the r-axis at A, giving rise to the angle A as marked. The line DB is drawn parallel to the r-axis so that the angle A is clearly equal to the angle formed by CBD.

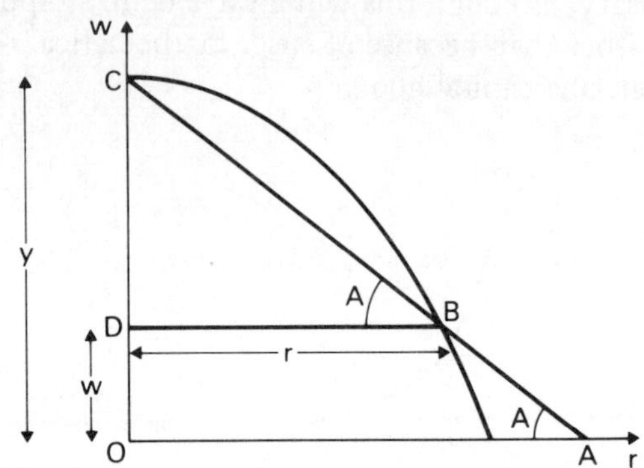

Diagram 5.6

In the figure, OC is marked equal to y, the net output per man. This follows from the simplifying assumptions made earlier, since, at the point where wages are a maximum and r = 0, net output per man is identical to wages per man. The maximum wage must equal the net output per man and so both equal OC. It follows that CD = y-w and the slope of the line CBA (measured by $\frac{CD}{DB}$) equals $\frac{y-w}{r}$ or k, OD equalling w and DB equalling r by definition of the coordinates at B.

At this stage, we can observe two things. First, that the value of capital will change even if the only other change in the economy is distributional (i.e., the number of machines remains constant — but their price changes). For, if we moved along the technique fpf to a different point of distribution than B, the slope of the line CBA would change accordingly. In diagram 5.6 for example, a higher value of capital is associated with a higher rate of profit. Conversely, if we took the fpf associated with diagram 5.4(b), a higher value of capital would be associated with a lower wage rate. Finally, for 4(c), the value of capital remains constant as r (and w change). This is an interesting case, because it is in a way the exception that proves the rule (or more exactly, the existence of the problem for the other cases). For the straight line fpf is the one in which the machine-labour ratios for the two production processes are the same. It follows that there can be no problem in evaluating corn relative to machines since, whatever the values taken by r and w, the price of corn relative to machines will always be the same, according to the *single* ratio in which inputs are used in the two production processes. For example, if machines are produced with twice the amount of machines *and* labour as are needed to produce corn then the price of machines must be twice the price of corn, irrespective of the values of w and r. In fact, this is the special case in which, from the point of view of production, it is as if there is only one good in the economy, precisely the case where the Cambridge critique will not arise. On the other hand, where $\frac{a}{\ell} \neq \frac{b}{n}$, as in the other cases considered, the value of capital does vary according to the values taken by r and w.

A second observation to be made at this stage is that there is no way of determining distribution from this single fpf. It merely represents an inverse relation between w and r but fixes neither. Yet this result and the perverse relationship between k and r for the fpf given by diagram 5.4(a) (it gives a positive relationship between k and r in contrast to the argument leading up to diagram 5.3) cannot be used to criticize the neo-classical model, since we have been restricted to a single technique of production whereas the neo-classical model relies upon a whole series of techniques associated with movement along the production function as capital is substituted for labour. We shall find, however, that these results are not invalidated by permitting a whole range of techniques and substitution between them.

Consider first the existence of one other alternative technique, comprising two production processes — one producing machines by machines and labour the other producing corn. For simplicity, we shall assume that the machinery for the second technique is incompatible with the method of producing corn with the first technique, that it is impossible to mix the production processes of different techniques. Now, associated with the second technique there will be a fpf as for the first. In general, the two fpf's when drawn together will cut each other as indicated in diagram 5.7(a), although one could be entirely inside the other, as in 7(b). Consider the second case first. It shows that at any given wage rate technique 2 will always sustain a higher rate of profit than technique 1. For example, at w_1, technique 1 would yield a rate of profit r_1, whilst technique 2 wourd yield r_2 greater than r_1, and the same is true whatever wage rate is chosen. Consequently, technique 1 will never be used, because whatever the wage rate is, technique 2 will give a higher rate of profit. In fact, this can be shown to be so if and only if technique 1 is inefficient in the sense that it uses both more machines and labour in the production of both machines and corn.

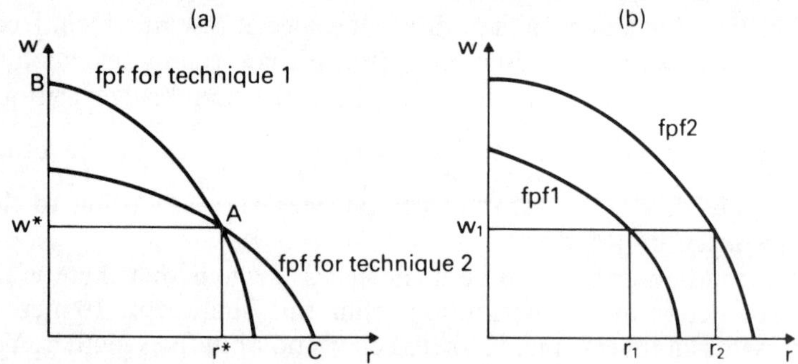

Diagram 5.7

The situation is more complicated for 7(a). There it can be seen that for a given wage rate, technique 1 will yield a higher rate of profit if $w > w^\star$ and technique 2 will do so if $w < w^\star$. When $w = w^\star$ each technique is equally profitable, yielding $r^\star$. From these considerations, it follows that technique 1 will be used if $w > w^\star$, and technique 2 will be used if $w < w^\star$, for these techniques will then respectively yield the higher rate of profit. The point A then is a watershed dividing the points at which technique 1 will be used from those at which technique 2 will be used. It is called a switch-point, for at the point switching or substituting one technique for another will be consistent with profit maximization.

We can now introduce the concept of the *economy* fpf by asking the question: given the two techniques, what is the maximum rate of profit for a given w? The answer is provided, as w varies, by our earlier arguments. The economy fpf is given by the outside of the two technique fpf's taken together, namely fpf 1 for $w > w^*$ and fpf 2 for $w < w^*$ by BAC. This curve, the outside of the two technique fpf's is called their envelope. It can be shown and it is intuitively obvious, that the economy fpf is downward sloping since each technique fpf is downward sloping.

So far we have only considered the economy fpf in the context of two techniques. In general, there will be a whole range of techniques that constitute the technology of the economy. Such a situation poses no more problems in principle for constructing the economy fpf. Again, it is simply the envelope of all the individual fpf's. As a result, the economy fpf lies outside each individual fpf, but each point on it must also lie on some technique fpf, as illustrated for a number of techniques in diagram 5.8.

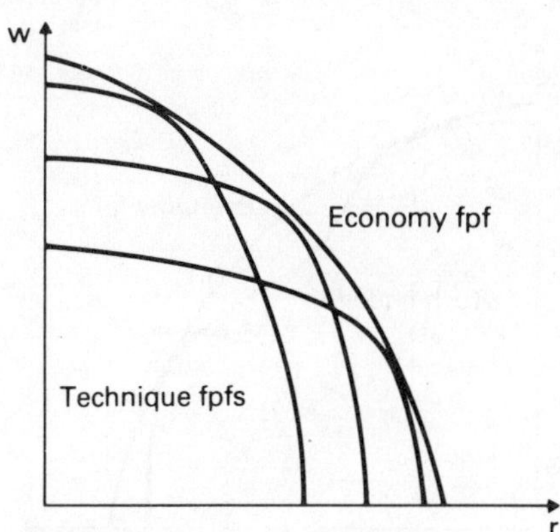

Diagram 5.8

It should be clear that the economy fpf is constructed from knowledge of the available production possibilities, in other words from information equivalent to knowledge of the available production function for the neo-classical one-sector model. In addition, knowledge of the technique in use corresponds to knowledge of the capital-labour ratio in the one-sector model. If the proposition of the one-sector model, that technology alone determines distribution, is to stand, it follows that knowledge of technology as a whole and the technique in use should determine distribution. From the knowledge of technology as a whole, however, we have the economy fpf, and from the particular technique in use, distribution can surely be deduced from the point at which the technique fpf touches the economy fpf? For example, for each of the techniques illustrated in diagram 5.8, a definite distribution follows from knowledge that that particular technique is in use. The values of w and r can be read off from the point at which the technique fpf concerned touches the economy fpf.

The foregoing argument is, however, erroneous for it presumes that each technique fpf only touches the economy fpf once. There is no reason why the economy fpf should not be touched by a technique fpf one or more times as illustrated in diagram 5.9. Then, it is impossible to determine distribution from technology alone, since associated with the technique is more than one possible distributional outcome. The result of neo-classical one-sector model is invalidated as a representation of multi-sector models.

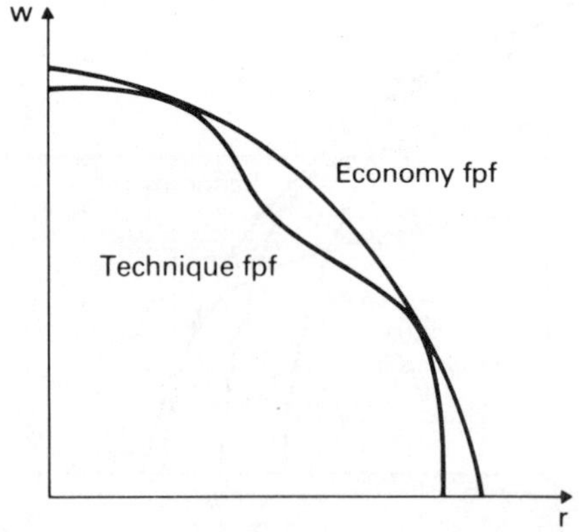

Diagram 5.9

We close this section by considering a necessary condition for a technique fpf to touch the economy fpf more than once, not because it is particularly important as such, but because it has received much attention in the literature. First, return to the economy with two techniques only as illustrated now in diagram 5.10. Here the two techniques cross twice so that there are switch-points at A and B. This is called re-switching. Consequently, in the absence of other techniques, technique 1 will be used at wage levels above that given at A, technique 2 will be used at wage levels between A and B, and technique 1 will again be the most profitable at wages below the level given by B. Already, we can see that the existence of reswitching is counter-intuitive to the neo-classical model, for it presumes that the same technique can be the most profitable at two different wages (and hence profit) rates. Nor should it be presumed that the existence of reswitching points in the economy fpf depends upon examining two techniques only. Exposition is eased, but there is no difficulty in principle in suggesting a continuum of other techniques that would yield an economy fpf which included the points A and B. We will now show that the non-correspondence between knowledge of technology, including the technique in use, and distributional relations depends upon the existence of reswitching.

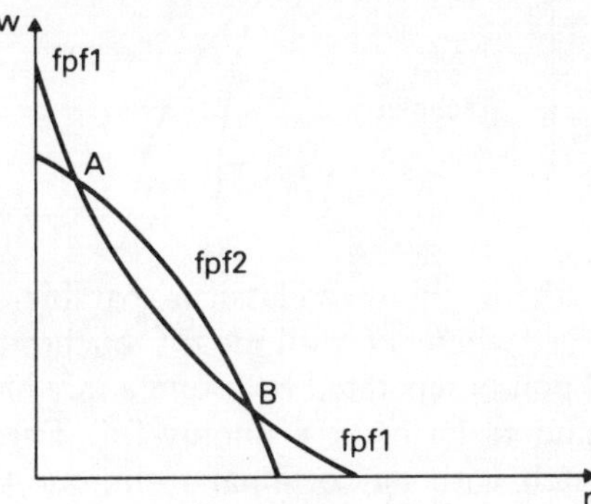

Diagram 5.10

From diagram 5.9 it has been shown that the problem for the neo-classical parable arises when a technique fpf touches the economy fpf more than once. In such circumstances, it is possible that the technique fpf is coincident with the economy fpf over a range as in diagram 5.11 between A and B. Then the knowledge that the technique concerned is in use would only permit us to deduce that distribution is determined somewhere within the range given by AB. Here indeterminancy of distribution does not require the existence of reswitching, but nor does this example correspond precisely to the neo-classical model. For the fact that no other technique switches with the one in use in the range DB denies the existence of substitutability in that range and it is substitutability between capital and labour (from one technique to another embodying different capital labour ratios) that is the basis of the neo-classical determination of distribution. Here we have a variation of the case illustrated in diagram 5.7(a) where there were only two as opposed to an infinite set of techniques. In these circumstance, neo-classical theory would expect to determine distribution only within limits. It corresponds to the case of the one-sector model where there is no continuous smooth substitution between capital and labour so that marginal products are themselves defined differently according to whether a factor input is added or taken away.

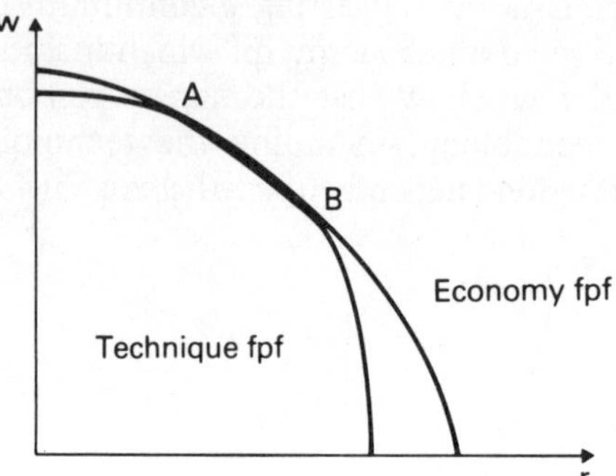

Diagram 5.11

Alternatively, then, the neo-classical parable only suffers a critique for the case where a technique fpf touches the economy fpf at two (or more) points separated by a range in which other technique fpfs touch and so form the economy fpf. These other techniques must reswitch with our original technique that yielded the distributional indeterminacy, as is illustrated in diagram 5.12 by the point C and the technique fpf associated with it. There is no other alternative for the technique fpf shown in part, that touches and forms the economy fpf at C.

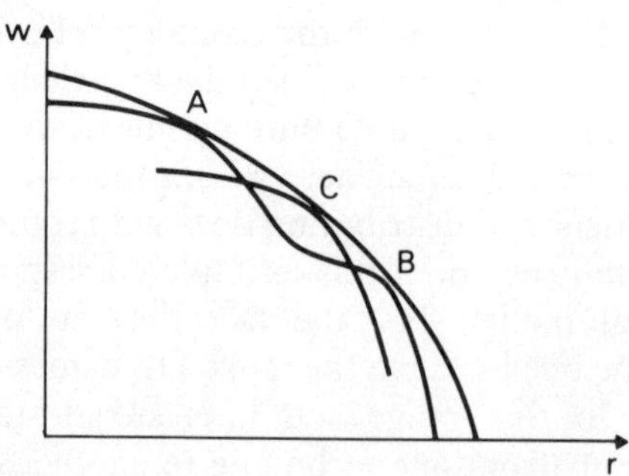

Diagram 5.12

These then are the technical results of the Cambridge critique of the neo-classical one-sector model. It has been shown that the one-sector model and the theoretical results associated with it cannot in general stand as a representation of a model with more than one good. The implications of this critique are considered in the following sections.

iii. The Significance of the Cambridge Critique for Distribution Theory

As it has been presented so far, the Cambridge critique has a relatively limited range of application for it has been preoccupied with the neo-classical one-sector model. By utilizing such a narrow base for its attack, the critique would appear to leave the majority of neo-classical economics unimpaired. Nevertheless, it has often been claimed that the critique destroys neo-classical economics as a whole and it is as well to examine the legitimacy of this claim.

One way in which the claim is presented is in terms of the illegitimacy of the concept of the marginal product of capital. As we have seen, to define the MPC, it is necessary to aggregate or index capital in some way and this creates irresolvable problems in the multi-sector economy. For if the index of capital is to be linked to a theory of the formation of the rate of profit, this variable has to be known to form the appropriate index of capital. But to argue that the marginal product of capital in aggregate is illegitimate is not to refute the concept of marginal product altogether. It quite clearly survives in terms defined by physical units, the incremental output of one good in response to the incremental input of another. The neo-classical one-sector model is legitimate in these terms as long as it is not taken as representative of multi-sector models, for the marginal product of capital can always be defined in physical terms. Similarly, if there exists a whole series of capital goods, the physical marginal product of each can be defined as in the one sector case. The difference is that these marginal products no longer yield a determination of the rate of profit, rather they will, for perfect competition, be equalized to the ratio of the input and output prices concerned. We have here restated the conclusion that in the multi-sector model technology alone cannot determine distribution.

But is this a proposition which is fundamentally at variance with the neo-classical tradition as a whole as opposed to the special instance of the one-sector model? The answer is in the negative. It is inscribed upon the statutes of neo-classical economics that prices and quantities are not determined by the technical conditions of production alone, but also by the relative marginal utilities of consumers for the goods that production can provide. Whether expressed in terms of supply and demand or the more sophisticated versions of general equilibrium theory, neo-classical economics has never relied upon technology alone to determine distribution.

Nevertheless, the retreat, if such it is rather than an advance of neo-classical economics from the one sector to the general equilibrium model, does pose further conceptual problems upon which the Cambridge critique has some bearing. Even when distribution is determined by the interaction of the conditions of production and consumer preferences, it depends upon the assumption of an initial endowment of factor inputs between individuals that forms the basis for the subsequent allocation of income. This presents two further problems. First, because all non-labour renumeration is drawn from the services of a given stock of initial endowments the neo-classical theory of distribution fails to draw a distinction between rent and profit as sources of revenue. Second, and leading on from the first problem, the neo-classical theory neither has an historical nor an economic explanation of the distribution of the stock of initial endowments.

To some extent, these problems of general equilibrium are a product of its timeless character, although the historical explanation of initial endowments is usually shrugged off as lying outside the subject matter of economics. The rate of profit cannot be explained without the passage of time in the model. Consequently, neo-classical economics can push the starting-point for initial endowments back a number of periods into the past, so that the general equilibrium includes the passage of time and the reproduction of resources period by period. The rate of profit is then explained in terms of the rewards of expanded production over time gained through the abstinence from current consumption. As a special case, neo-classical theory can push the starting-point for initial endowments back indefinitely into the infinite past. This gives the impression of doing away with the problem by constructing steady state balanced growth paths that have always existed and will always exist. But this infinite regress is no more an explanation of initial endowments than man is borne of man is an explanation of the evolution of the human species.

In these terms, the Cambridge critique can be seen to be extremely weak. It draws up the economy fpf and defies neo-classical economics to deduce distributional relations from this together with the knowledge of the technique in use. The predictable response from a neo-classical theorist would be that distribution can only be determined on the basis of the additional knowledge of consumers' preferences, in particular for the pattern of consumption over time. At given rates of profit and wages, each individual will form plans to work and save, yielding for the economy as a whole aggregate supplies of and demands for labour and capital goods. In equilibrium these must be equalized yielding another relation between w and r, which with the economy fpf allows the economy to be determined.

What we have shown is that the Cambridge critique does not and cannot take as its point of departure from neo-classical economics the existence and correction of logical or conceptual inconsistencies in the latter. What it does do is to reject the formation of the extra equation determining distribution outlined in the previous paragraph and to substitute an alternative procedure. Rather than relying upon the aggregate effect of individual intertemporal preference to determine the point of distribution on the economy fpf, an appeal is usually made to class struggle over the level of wages, but other procedures are possible (such as the determination of the rate of profit as the rate of interest according to the supply of and demand for money).

So much for the differences between neo-classical economics and its Cambridge critique. What is more significant is the elements of analysis that they share in common. Each depends upon an exogenously given set of technical relations that are intended to incorporate the conditions of production. From these are formed the necessary logical relations between prices, wages and profits on the basis of perfect competition (to equalize these) and profit maximization by entrepreneurs. Consequently, it can be seen that the Cambridge critique of the neo-classical *one-sector* production function is precisely that, a simple criticism of the reliance upon a one-sector model. Everything else remains unchanged on the production side. In effect, the Cambridge *critique* is a misnomer. It is not a criticism but a *reconstruction* of neo-classical production theory by a generalization of the simple one-sector model to many sectors. As a result, the critique can simply be absorbed into the mainstream of neo-classical economics rather than forming a radical rupture with it.

For these reasons the critique as such does not lead to solutions to the problems that it poses for neo-classical economics. It does not confront the problem of the origins of initial endowments. For like much neo-classical theory, its analysis is of steady-state equilibrium paths that extend indefinitely both backward and forward in time. (Those descriptions of movements along the economy fpf in the previous section give a misleading impression. For they do not refer to the dynamics of the economy but to the comparative statics of different steady-state equilibrium paths). Nor can the critique provide any answer to the prior question of the explanation of the existence of wages and profits. This question is logically prior since it is necessary to know that we are seeking the origins of the initial endowments of means of production *as capital* and not simply as the inputs to a technically defined production process. Knowledge of the social conditions necessary for profits to be formed in the economy is a prerequisite for an understanding of the historical process whereby these conditions were created. The critique, like neo-classical economics, simply presumes the existence of profits, wages and prices and so can only explain the existence of profits on the basis of the fact that wages do not absorb all the net product. With this neo-classical economics can agree, but it has another feather to its cap — the marginal utility of consumption over time to determine the quantitative allocation of net product to wages and profits. In response to this all that is offered is not a critique, but a theory of distributional struggle between classes that neo-classical theory can in any case accommodate in terms of a theory of bargaining and duopoly, that is of classes treated as conflicting individuals.

In short, the implications of the critique for distribution theory are shown to be negligible. It does not break from the theoretical terrain occupied by neo-classical economics, indeed it is a reconstruction of that school's theory of production for a multi-sector economy. Nor can it be said to pose and answer questions that negate and explain the inadequacies of neo-classical theory. For like neo-classical theory it takes as given the existence of the categories of capitalist society and consequently must leave them unexplained together with their specific historical origin.

iv. The Significance of the Cambridge Critique for Empirical Estimation

It has been the argument of the previous section that far from breaking with neo-classical economics, the Cambridge critique can be considered more or less a branch of that school of economics! This conclusion will leave many economists on both sides of the controversy both astounded and dissatisfied. For those neo-classical economists who have struggled violently against the critique and its conclusions can scarcely be anything but astonished at the suggestion that it lies within their own mode of theorizing. Perhaps even more uncomfortable will be the proponents of the critique who consider that their analysis announces the demise of neo-classical economics rather than a contribution to it.

However, to correct the impression that may have been given to the reader that the critique has no significance except to generalize the neo-classical one-sector model, it can be shown that the critique has devastating implications for one area of orthodox economics, namely for that econometric work based on the existence of aggregate production functions. But first consider an argument that is made in response to the Cambridge critique, for an examination of it will reveal the theoretical wilderness in which neo-classical economics is often located. Because the critique depends upon the existence of reswitching, it is argued that its validity or relevance depends upon the existence of reswitching in the real world, that is upon an empirical question which is open to investigation by examination of the real world. Needless to say, for practical reasons that will become clear, nobody has ever investigated whether reswitching actually does exist or not, least of all those who argue it is the most relevant question. Rather the economic intuitions associated with the one-sector model continue to exercise their hold over what can only be described as the weaker minds in the neo-classical tradition.

Why is it that the significance of reswitching cannot be reduced to an empirical question? An answer can be given at many different levels. At the most general, the question itself can be seen to be ridiculous, for there is no such thing as a purely empirical question, since the data do not simply exist in the real world. They are produced on the basis of certain theoretical, although not necessarily coherent, preconceptions and equally can only be assessed on the basis of a theoretical system. Indeed, it can be seen that the reduction of reswitching to an empirical question involves the simple fallacy of identifying the *thought* concepts of the economic theory concerned with a real existence. More specifically, how are we to set about testing whether reswitching exists or not when the theoretical system in which the question arises presumes among other things, constant returns to scale, fixed and exogenously given technical relations and no externalities in production? This is not a question of the 'realism' or otherwise of these assumptions as such, for realism is itself not simply an empirical question. Rather, it is a question of a necessary divorce between reality and the concepts that attempt to reproduce it in thought. Thus, the significance of reswitching can never be simply an empirical question. It is a theoretical result that exposes the limitations of the neo-classical one-sector model on its own terms.

So far, the reduction of the Cambridge critique to an empirical question has been condemned solely for its understanding of the possibility of a relationship between a given theory and an exogenously given set of data with which to assess the theory. But the data itself must be produced and this is not simply a matter of employing a sufficient number of civil servants in the statistics division. For even putting aside the illegitimate identification of the theoretical concepts with the supposed real world, the data necessary to test for the existence of reswitching include all the possible techniques of production that may be used. But the theory itself produces the result that the only techniques in use will be the most profitable ones so that it will be more or less impossible to produce data on all techniques since the real world itself does not produce these data (except in the minds of the entrepreneurs who reject the less profitable techniques). No wonder that the empirical question of the significance of reswitching has not been empirically investigated!

But it is perhaps unjust to belabour those neo-classical economists, who shrug off the Cambridge critique as an empirical question, for their naive understanding of the relationship between theory and reality. For this is a common deficiency within the neo-classical tradition. Nevertheless, the "carry on regardless" brigade of econometricians do commit the most profound errors even within the bounds of the neo-classical mode of reason. For where they reduce the significance of the Cambridge critique for distribution *theory* to an empirical question concerning reswitching, they also perpetrate a sleight of hand by applying the same principle to econometric investigation. As we shall see, this is illegitimate for the invalidity of the empirical investigations does not depend upon the occurrence of reswitching.

Let us begin however with an instance of reswitching to give a flavour of the problems that are created for empirical investigation that rely upon an aggregation of physical capital goods. In diagram 5.13, it is presumed that the *technique* fpf illustrated is the most profitable at both A and B for the economy as a whole. It follows if we compare the economy at B with it at A, that it has a higher value of capital (slope of CB as opposed to CA), higher profit rate and equal output per man given by OC since the same technique is in use for A and B. Now neo-classical empirical work generally indexes capital at current prices to form the value of capital. Taking all these factors together, the neo-classical model would have to conclude that technology as a whole had changed in the movement from A to B since the relationships embodied in figures 1-3 for a given technology can be seen not to hold (y should increase for increasing k, and r should decrease). In fact, not only technology but even the technique in use has remained invariant. The beauty of this neo-classical method of empirical investigation is that it would use the observations associated with these movements to measure the extent to which technology had changed; it would measure in this case technological decay when the only change is a distributional one.

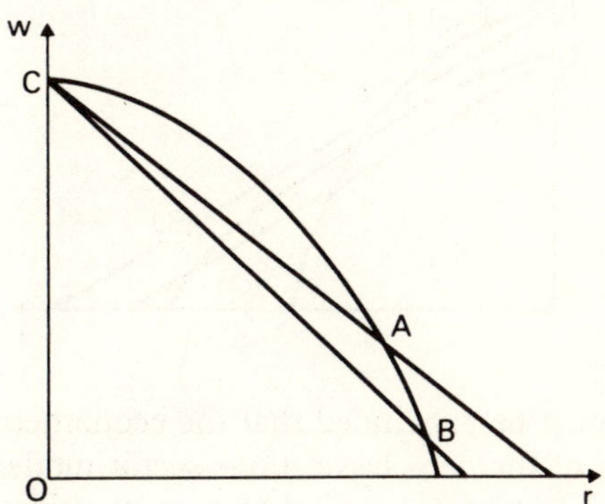

Diagram 5.13

In the foregoing example, reswitching has been assumed, since a technique fpf has been the most profitable at two different levels of wages, but this is not necessary to invalidate the neo-classical use of aggregate production functions. Rather it brings out very clearly the source of the error. In general, a movement along the economy fpf will represent the combination of two effects, the change in technique and the change in distributional relations, *each* of which influences the value of capital k which is a price times a quantity. However, the neo-classical one-sector model is unable to accommodate changes in the price of capital precisely because it is a one-sector model. Accordingly any pure change in distribution which affects the price (and so value) of capital without affecting its quantity must be measured by the one-sector model as a change in technology. This is what the example relying upon reswitching brings out most clearly. More generally, the problem does not disappear without reswitching, it just involves the more complicated interaction of quantity and price effects. For example, in diagram 5.14, let us suppose that technique 1 is the most profitable for the economy at A and technique 2 at C. Then both techniques yield respectively at these points the same value of capital given by the slope of the lines AB and CD, presumed equal. But between these points both y and r change so that the neo-classical one-sector model would have to measure a change in technology, not just in technique, which would combine the effects of a distributional and technique change in the movement from A to C.

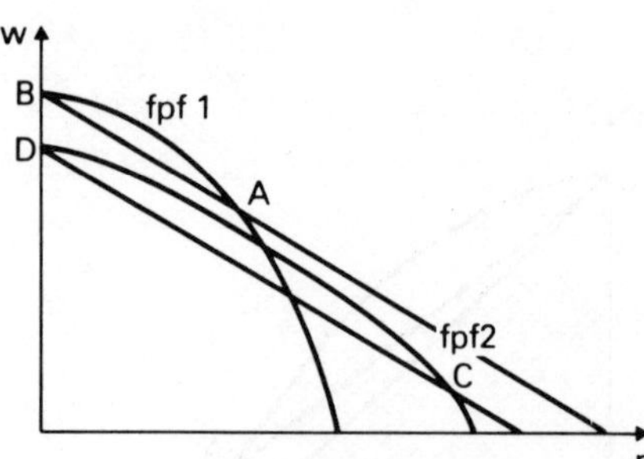

Diagram 5.14

In short, it must be concluded that the econometric work that is in the tradition of the neo-classical one-sector model, more specifically that which aggregates capital at current prices, is incoherent since it attempts to measure the two dimensions of change associated with technology and distribution with a one dimensional rule. The extent of this incoherence should not be underestimated. It applies to any measurement of production functions, for example in the measurement of technical progress or human capital as contributors to growth. On the other hand, the destructive implications of the Cambridge critique should not be overestimated. It does not involve an abandonment of empirical investigation of neo-classical models altogether, only those that require aggregation at current prices. Just as the Cambridge critique of the neo-classical theory of distribution is not so much met as absorbed by its general equilibrium theory, so the implications of the critique for neo-classical econometrics may be accommodated by the estimation of general equilibrium systems of simultaneous equations or technical conditions in physical rather than price terms. Precisely these points are recognized by the best neo-classical practitioners of econometrics, just as their more theoretically oriented compatriots incorporate the Cambridge critique into a general equilibrium analysis.

One final question remains: if the neo-classical one-sector model is an exercise in theorizing that leads to invalid propositions and empirical investigation *on its own terms*, why does it persist? One answer can be given in terms of the inertia of the economics profession, the defence of its received doctrines and modes of thinking and teaching. Whilst an element of truth is to be found in this explanation, it is too general and has no specific relation to the particular incoherent mode of theorizing under consideration. Nor does it explain the genesis of the doctrine even if it does explain its persistence. A more specific explanation is provided by the confusion created by the forms assumed by capital, coupled though it may be to the incoherence and obstinacy of some neo-classical reasoning. For the aggregation of physical capital at current prices is not some ideal abstraction but actually corresponds to the form assumed by capital as it is advanced to purchase inputs. Whilst it must at this stage be advanced in the form of money, a fact that escapes the neo-classical theory and its Cambridge critique, the process of aggregation is nevertheless no fiction and feeds the intuition that it is legitimate to utilise an index for capital and its money value in particular. But this index is itself used to represent the role played by capital at another point in its circuit, namely in production. The neo-classical confusion comes from running together in its concept of homogeneous capital, its existence as money as opposed to its existence in production. At least then a recognition of the existence of these two forms of capital is implicit within its analysis. The apparently superior theory embodied in general equilibrium (and the Cambridge critique) is only gained at the expense of excluding any connection to the money-form of capital.

Further Reading

A classical non-mathematical presentation of the Cambridge critique is J. Robinson, 'The Production Function and the Theory of Capital', *Review of Economic Studies*, XXI, 1953-54. The graphical techniques utilized for exposition are taken from A. Bhaduri, 'On the Significance of Recent Controversies in Capital Theory: A Marxian View', *Economic Journal*, vol. 79, 1969. For an analysis of the affinity between the Cambridge critique theory and neo-classical economics, see B. Rowthorn, 'Vulgar Economy', *New Left Review*, 86, 1974. A survey of contributions to the critique is to be found in G. Harcourt, *Some Cambridge Controversies in the Theory of Capital*, Cambridge University Press, 1972, but this book is difficult to follow unless its contents are already understood. A more presentable but less detailed discussion is A. Sen, 'On Some Debates in Capital Theory', *Economica*, 1974.

6

The Labour Theory of Value

i. What is the Labour Theory of Value?

In the history of economic thought, there is one idea that dominates orthodox thinking, and much thinking in the Marxist tradition besides, concerning the labour theory of value: that, whatever significance such a definition has, the theory takes the value of a good to be the labour-time that has been used in producing it. Then, with this as starting point, the validity and usefulness of the theory is evaluated in terms of a number of questions: how well does the labour theory explain prices, what is its status as a theory of distribution, what is its positive explanatory contribution as opposed to its ethical or normative content? In these terms, assessments are made of the labour theory of value and its supposed bedfellow, Marxist economics.

If the value of a good, as opposed to its price, is defined in terms of the labour time required to produce it, then this labour-time can in turn be divided into two portions. The first, which we shall denote as living labour ℓ, is the immediate input of labour into the work process. In contrast, the portion of constant capital c is the amount of labour that has already been exerted to produce the physical inputs that are used by living labour in the current production process. How c is worked out need not concern us unduly, although two alternatives present themselves. The first involves tracing back through time and adding up every labour input that has contributed to the production of the constant capital. The second is to set up an accounting system that allocates values to goods and is solved mathematically. For example, suppose that $\frac{1}{2}$ unit of corn is used with 1 unit of labour to produce 1 unit of corn. Then the value of corn is the 1 unit of living labour plus the value of $\frac{1}{2}$ a unit of corn. But to produce $\frac{1}{2}$ of corn requires $\frac{1}{4}$ of corn and

$\frac{1}{2}$ labour, which in turn requires $\frac{1}{8}$ corn and $\frac{1}{4}$ of labour,...... Consequently, the value of corn is $1 + \frac{1}{2} + \frac{1}{4} + ..$ which as a geometric progression sums to 2. Alternatively, if the value of corn is t, then $\frac{t}{2} + 1 = t$, since the value of inputs (1 unit of labour and $\frac{1}{2}$ unit of corn) must equal the value of output (1 unit of corn). Again, this yields $t = 2$. In either case, the result in more general terms and for the more complicated cases in which there is a whole series of different inputs and outputs is that $t = c + \ell$.

For a capitalist economy, in which wages are paid as a means of obtaining labour inputs, the element of living labour ℓ can be further broken down. If the value of the bundle of wage goods is v, then a surplus value s equal to the difference between ℓ and v will be left over to form profits. Thus, $t = c + v + s$ where $\ell = v + s$. Now, if we take values as a direct determinant of prices p, then $p = c + \ell$. This implies that prices are determined quite independently of the distribution of net product between capital and labour, or, what is the same thing, independently of the distribution of the worker's living labour to the capitalist as opposed to himself. For, if s increases v decreases by the same amount, and vice-versa, leaving ℓ and p unchanged.

On the other hand, in a capitalist economy surplus value is distributed to capitalists in the form of profit. Moreover, just as workers' wages will tend to be equalized by competition in the labour market, so the rate of profit will be equalized by competition between capitalists. This implies that the price of a good is comprised of wage costs, other input costs and a uniform rate of profit r on these. Accordingly, $p = (c + v)(1 + r)$, assuming that wages are paid at the beginning of the period so that they count as a capital advance.

These calculations yield two different determinations of prices, one according to the labour time of production, the other according to the principle of distribution, profits in proportion to capital advanced. For them to be compatible it must follow that for each sector

$$c + v + s = (c + v)(1 + r)$$

This equation reduces to $s = (c + v)\,r$ or

$$r = \frac{s}{c + v} = \frac{s/v}{c/v + 1}$$

Now, r and s/v are uniform across the economy, the latter being so because labour mobility will ensure equalized wages for a given working day and so an equalized division of ℓ into s and v. But from this it follows that c/v must be uniform across the economy also, otherwise the last equation would not hold for every sector as it must by derivation. The only exception is the case in which both r and s/v are zero. For then the last equation holds, as well as the preceding one, since r = s = 0.

The conclusion to be drawn from this analysis is that the labour theory of value is an adequate theory of price formation in two special cases only. The first is when workers receive all net product so that profits are zero, the second is when the ratio of capital used as physical means of production to capital advanced as wages is the same in every sector. As both of these conditions are to be considered unnecessarily restrictive, the conclusion is drawn that the labour theory of value must be rejected as a theory of price formation.

The rejection of the labour theory of value as a theory of price formation is not however necessarily an absolute rejection of a theory based on labour-time. For, as the reader may be aware, Marx for example based his analysis of capitalism on values but argued that prices would systematically diverge from these. In arithmetical terms, Marx argued as follows. Suppose one capital is composed of 60 c and 40 v, whilst another is made up of 40 c and 60 v. Then each capital must receive the same profit, since each is a value advanced of 100, but each does not produce the same surplus value. For suppose that s/v is equal to unity, then 40s will be produced by the first capital and 60s by the second. Taken together the two capitals earn 100s and this must, after exchange, be distributed equally between them. Accordingly, the price of the products of each must be 150, this representing the original capital advanced of 100 together with a mark-up of 50 per cent, the average rate of profit formed from the total surplus produced 100s relative to the total capital advanced 100c + 100v = 200.

More generally, Marx's solution can in technical terms be derived as follows. Let C, V and S represent the sums of c, v and s respectively over the whole economy. Then the average rate of profit is formed as $r = \frac{S}{C + V}$. As a result, individual prices are formed as $p = (c + v)(1 + r)$. In general, these prices will diverge from their respective values. Those with a c/v higher than the average will exchange at prices above their values (as for the capital

60c + 40v above with value 140 and price 150), whereas those with a lower c/v than average will have prices below their values (40c + 60v having value 160 but price 150).

In Marx's derivation of prices from values, it is no longer concluded that prices equal values since profit is appropriated according to capital advanced. Nevertheless, his derivation is incorrect in general since it paradoxically both depends upon the assumption that commodities exchange at their values and the conclusion that they do not. For consider capital advanced, c + v. This is estimated in value terms, whereas the advance is made in money to purchase inputs at prices that we are about to conclude diverge from values. This paradox, or more exactly inconsistency, can be pointed out in another way. Because the inputs are not transformed to reflect capital advanced in prices rather than values, it follows by considering the economy as a whole that the goods that are sold as outputs, at prices of production that diverge from values, are bought as inputs at prices that equal values. A clear inconsistency since buying and selling prices are necessarily equal for any transaction.

So Marx made a mistake, but incidentally one of which he was aware although he never corrected it. As a result, it can be shown that Marx's derivation of prices from values are not all that is in error. In addition, his calculation of the rate of profit as the ratio of surplus value to capital advanced is also wrong. For the rate of profit is the ratio of two quantities calculated in money-price terms, and as we have seen the formation of the rate of profit involves the divergence of prices from values. Consequently S/(C + V) will not in general equal the same ratio of surplus to capital advanced calculated on the basis of prices of production.

But to show Marx's error is not to invalidate either the labour theory of value nor the totality of Marxist economics. Indeed, the error is easily remedied by calculating capital advanced as well as commodities sold in prices rather than values so that both inputs and outputs are bought and sold at prices that diverge from values. That this can be done is beyond dispute. What is more controversial is the status of such a procedure as an economic theory. Clearly judgement on this question will depend upon the criteria that are used to assess theory and, by implication, the questions that are posed and answered within the theory. As we have presented the labour theory of value so far, it has been entirely in terms dictated by orthodox economic thinking: what is the relationship between prices and values, the latter defined as the labour-time required for production. But contrary to that thinking, Marx's value theory was not predominantly concerned with this question. It is time to redress the balance.

ii. Marx's Value Theory

It is important to begin by stressing that Marx's value theory is not predominantly concerned with the adding up of labour-time to form values and then investigating their quantitative relationship to prices, the mode of analysis presented in the previous section. Rather than justifying the concept of value on the basis of the results to which it *leads* in price or distribution theory, Marx wished to demonstrate that value is a concept that has itself to be explained in terms of its correspondence to relations that exist in the real world. The relevant questions are what is value and why does it exist, for in contrast to prices, for example, values are not a simple observational fact of everyday life. Goods in a shop window have their prices displayed to the world, the same cannot and could not be true for their value. Consequently, there is a certain methodological inconsistency when prices and values are introduced simultaneously at the outset into an analysis of the relationship between them. For the two concepts have a different status, one requires justification for its existence, the other does not.

Nor should it be presumed that a definition of value is a substitute for an explanation of it. That value is the labour-time of production presumes that all labour has been reduced to a homogeneous standard. This presents a number of problems, some of which have implicitly come to the fore in the previous section whilst demonstrating how values would be calculated theoretically. The formation of values out of the summation of past and living labour presumes, even in the one good corn world, that all labours past and present are not only commensurate but also count equally time for time. The method that calculates values for a many-product world presumes the same result for labours of different qualities in the sense of tailoring as opposed to carpentry etc. as well as for labours of different skills within the same sphere of production.

In the orthodox understanding of the labour theory of value, the position of reducing all labour to a homogeneous standard is solved by a mental construction alone. It is assumed that the reduction can be made as an approximation to reality and as a means for examining the legitimacy of the labour theory of value in its purest simplicity as a theory of price. Consequently, a number of objections can be made to the theory quite irrespective of its performance in the last regard. If the theory is simply an approximation, then it is invalidated by those closer approximations that do not rest on such restrictive assumptions. Further, in so far as these assumptions are unrealistic, demanding as they do that the world contains a homogeneous labour force or something equivalent to it, the labour theory of value becomes a construct of the imagination, like religion purely metaphysical.

These are indeed valid objections to the labour theory of value against which they are aimed, but they are completely irrelevant to Marx's value theory. For Marx did not base his concept of value on a mental construct removed from the real world and requiring all sorts of arbitrary assumptions. Rather, his argument is based upon the fact that the reduction of all types of labour to a common standard is a product of the real world itself, not it must be added for all societies but for those in which commodity production is predominant. In a commodity producing society, all different types of labour — what Marx called concrete labour — and labours of different skills are brought into equivalence with each other through exchange. Consequently, the price relations between commodities is the form in which an equivalence is established between different concrete labours, the means by which these are reduced to homogeneous labour that counts as value, what Marx called abstract labour.

An examination of the labour theory of value in this way has a number of important implications. First, it suggests that the theory is not simply a quantitative aggregation of labour times to form values, but a theory of the relationship between the performance of heterogeneous concrete labours in production and their commensuration through exchange as commodities. In other words, Marx's theory is concerned with the form of value in exchange, how concrete labours which exist in all societies also take on the character of abstract labour and values in commodity producing societies.

Second, then, this concept of value has definite historical roots in two different senses. It both draws its existence from particular economic epochs (commodity producing societies) and is nonsensical for others, precisely because it is a theory of the form of value. We can note by contrast that the labour theory of value based simply on the aggregation of labour time can be considered ahistorical in both these senses. It involves a mental construct to dismiss the problems of different skills and types of labour, a mental construct which can in principle be applied to all societies irrespective of whether the products of labour take the form of commodities or not (i.e. irrespective of whether concrete labours are simultaneously abstract labours and hence values).

Since Marx's value theory is specific to a particular historical epoch, it is thereby necessarily a theory that consciously embodies certain social relations peculiar to that epoch. It captures the relations that bind human labours together in a commodity-producing society, highlighting both a production and a social division of labour geared towards exchange.

Third, as demanded earlier in this section, values have a theoretical status distinct from prices. Because prices are the form of values in exchange and the means by which values are formed, they have an immediate appearance and by the same token values do not. Consequently this poses the question of how values become prices, not in a simple numerical sense, but in terms of the economic relations that unite the multitude of specific types of labour in production to the distribution and exchange of products. If we assume, as was done in the previous section, that values and prices both exist, and only seek to derive the latter numerically from the former then we cannot pose this question. We do not ask *how* do values become prices, in the sense of the price formation of abstract labour and values out of concrete labours, but *whether* values existing in the abstract alone as homogeneous labour have a numerical relation to prices that is of interest by some criterion or other. It follows that Marx's value theory addresses itself to different questions than those posed by orthodox notions of the labour theory of value and so can only be assessed partially within its terms of reference.

Finally, an implication of Marx's value theory is that prices diverge from value not only qualitatively but also quantitatively. The theory poses the need to analyse the relations by which values are formed in exchange as prices, so that there can be no presumption that the two are numerically equal. In addition, the objections to the labour theory of value that it relies upon unjustified assumptions such as the homogeneity of labour are quite irrelevant as far as Marx's value theory is concerned. For, these assumptions are not made in Marx's value theory and nor are others that would appear to be necessary for the labour theory of value, such as constancy of technology. The reduction of all labours to a homogeneous standard is not an assumption that disregards the complexities of the real world. It is a product of the world of commodity production that demands further analysis, and this is precisely what Marx undertakes in his political economy, in his analysis of the accumulation, exchange and distribution of value.

The conclusion of this section is that orthodox considerations of Marx's theory of value have suffered from an erroneous and almost uniform identification of it with a labour theory of value simply based on labour-time. To some extent this can be explained by a careless reading of *Capital's* three volumes. For there, in the first two volumes, Marx does indeed proceed on the basis of commodities exchanging at their values. It is only in the third volume that he considers the systematic divergence of prices from values. Consequently, it is concluded that Marx's analysis in the third volume invalidates that of the earlier volumes.

Here, however, there is a misunderstanding of Marx's exposition that is not unconnected with the misunderstanding of his value theory. Before the derivation of prices from values can be considered, the production of surplus value has to be analysed. For, without surplus value there are no profits, and without profits there would be no systematic deviations of prices from values. Just as earlier we saw that prices and values are categories with different theoretical status, so the same applies to profits which have an immediate existence as opposed to surplus value which does not. Surplus value cannot therefore be taken to exist, it must be shown to exist as a result of the specific social relations associated with capitalism. It is this, why and how does capital lead to the production of surplus value, that predominantly concerns Marx in Volume I of Capital. This explains the preoccupation with capital as self-expanding value, M-C-M′, and the distinction between labour and labour-power with the characterization of the latter as a commodity as a specific necessity for capitalism. The analysis is based upon exchange at values, because otherwise it would presume an understanding of the quantitative distribution of surplus value prior to an analysis of its prodution. In Volume II of *Capital*, Marx only analyses the qualitative processes whereby surplus value is distributed through the exchange of commodities, for which exchange at values suffices. It is the quantitative division of surplus value between capitals, or more exactly the relations by which surplus value is formed in exchange as the profit part of price that is the concern of Volume III's treatment of the transformation problem.

iii. The Labour Theory of Value in the History of Economic Thought

The existence of value, as a consequence of the historically specific conditions in which products take the form of commodities, has an important bearing on the development of economic theory. Indeed, it is only with the emergence of commodity production that economics itself develops as an intellectual discipline. For those in any way familiar with the history of economic thought, it cannot have escaped notice that the labour theory of value was a central organizing principle at the very origins of economic theory. Usually this is explained with neo-classical hindsight as the result of the subject's infancy. An oversimplified (labour) cost of production theory remained to be perfected by the complement of a demand theory based on utility. But if we probe a little deeper, the rise (and subsequent decline) of the labour theory of value can be more satisfactorily explained.

With the emergence of commodity production, we have seen that not only products as things come to be exchanged but also that these commodities exchange as the products of labour. In other words, theorists were confronted with explaining the new phenomenon, that human labours were not simply in equivalence but were being brought into equivalence with each other through exchange. In this light, it is not surprising that the labour theory of value should emerge as a reflection of economic developments. For, the more commodity production, that is production specifically for the market as opposed to the sale of an accidental or fortuitous surplus, encroached upon production for immediate consumption, the more producers were faced with the necessity of comparing their labour with the standard set by the market. Such comparisons were embodied in the decision of whether it be better to buy or produce a particular commodity, the former alternative requiring the production of some other commodity to sell in exchange. In contrast, once the specialization and the generalization of commodity production had developed, the conscious comparison of labour-times is severely circumscribed, particularly as these developments are associated with capitalism for which the producers (wage-labourers) have no control over what they produce. The capitalists, who do have this control, base their calculations on money costs rather than on the labour-time of others. As a result, the appeal to theorists of an economics based on labour-time is severely limited. Thus, it is not the existence of commodity production per se that induces the labour theory of value, although we have argued earlier that Marx's value theory is based upon the existence of commodity production. Rather, it is the process of the emergence of commodity production that leads to the labour theory of value, just as it is the development of capitalist commodity production that leads to its demise.

These remarks are borne out if we consider the history of the labour theory of value in slightly more detail. Take first the bases on which values have been calculated. For the physiocratic school, it was labour-time engaged in agriculture that was the sole source of value, a clear reflection of the predominance of this sector as commodity exchange developed. On the other hand, the mercantilist school identified exchange activity as the creator of value, a reflection of the role played by commerce in the consolidation of international trading relations. For classical political economy, associated say with Smith and Ricardo, value was based on the labour-time exercised in productive activity in general, and this reflected the generalization of commodity production to many sectors. Now, it could be argued that the various schools simply proposed theories that supported particular economic interests, argicultural, commercial and industrial respectively. This is undoubtedly true, but the theories concerned were not a dishonest fabrication with that purpose in mind, but a necessary response to the particular economic developments with which they were confronted.

For our purposes, the value theory of classical political economy is most interesting since it is generalized to include all commodity production. Smith's elementary demonstration of labour time is most instructive, for he returns to that rude state of society in which each producer is free to hunt deer and beaver as he chooses. The two products will exchange at the ratio of the times it takes to catch them. Paradoxically, Smith refers to a society in which there is no exchange, for each producer can hunt as needs require, to explain the ratio at which products do exchange in that society! This inconsistency can be explained in terms of Smith's projecting the characteristics of the commodity producing society onto the 'rude' non-commodity producing society from which it was emerging at his time of writing. Nevertheless, Smith ultimately rejected a value theory based on labour-time. For whilst it could apply to the rude society, it was inapplicable to a capitalist society in which profits and rents formed component parts of prices when added to input costs. Smith's rejection of value theory, however, only came after a series of developments in his thought, each corresponding to a new understanding of what constituted capitalism.

To begin with Smith characterized a capitalist as an independent commodity producer. In this case, with no labourers to exploit, the rate of profit would be zero. Indeed, a completely inappropriate understanding of capitalism has been utilized, with the use of a stock of means of production being confused with capitalist production. However, with a zero rate of profit, the labour theory of value as a theory of price is valid, as has been seen in the first section. Smith then proceeded to characterize a capitalist as an employer of wage labour. Whilst nearer the mark, Smith excluded the use of physical means of production by the labourers. The result is a capitalism for which the organic composition of capital is equal in each sector (to zero) so that once again the labour theory of value holds as a theory of price. But once Smith is forced through capital's own development to recognize that the organic composition is non-zero, the labour theory of value is simply abandoned in favour of a theory that forms wages, profits, and rents independently and adds them in the appropriate proportions to form prices.

It was against this rejection of the labour theory of value that Ricardo reacted. An implication that could be drawn from Smith's analysis is that an increase in wages would lead to an increase in the prices of all commodities according to the amount of labour employed in the production of each. For Ricardo, the labour theory of value would associate a compensating decline in profits with an increase in wages so that prices would remain unaltered. His analysis stumbled, however, across the differences in the organic compositions of capital for which commodities no longer exchanged at their values. To this Ricardo had a response. Those commodities that have a composition of capital above the average would decrease in price with an increase in wages since the increased wage cost would be more than compensated for by the decreased profits that would accrue on the capital intensive costs as a result of the decrease in the rate of profit. The opposite conclusion would hold for a commodity produced with a composition of capital below the average or for a decline in wages (increase in the rate of profit).

From this point, Ricardo became preoccupied with the problem of determining what constituted the average commodity, the invariable standard of value whose composition of capital was such that its price remained unaffected by distributional changes and against which the changes in prices of commodities with different compositions could be measured. (Of course, if the invariable standard is not itself the money commodity, then its price would change with wage decreases, for example, but in inverse proportion to the composition of capital used in the production of the money commodity). Ricardo seemed less concerned with the implications that his theory had for the labour theory of value. What he had shown was that the labour theory of value is inconsistent with a theory of price based on profit according to capital advanced. The principle of value according to labour time had to be modified according to the different compositions of capital (and also for the different times taken by production processes which would affect the time for which capital was advanced and therefore the profit to be added to form price). Nevertheless, Ricardo remained doggedly committed to the labour theory of value, despite the fact that it produced its own inconsistencies, arguing that deviations of prices from values would not be unduly significant. Such a recourse to an empirical sleight of hand is hardly satisfactory theoretically nor deserving of more comment. More interesting is a closer scrutiny of the inconsistency involved in Ricardo's value theory, for the particular fashion in which it is resolved or *reproduced* determines the future differences between one school of economic thought or another. Nor should it be presumed that an economic theory that reproduces the inconsistency is in some sense to be considered inferior to one that does not. For, whilst consistency is a requirement that should be satisfied by any theory, there are other requirements also and there is no reason to suppose that these should always be subordinated to consistency. Indeed, it is quite possible to envisage a theory of the purest consistency but of complete irrelevance and also one of inconsistency in collaboration with the deepest insights.

In the broadest terms, Ricardo's inconsistency consists of the simultaneous application of two conflicting principles, calculation of value according to labour time and calculation of value according to capital advanced. For Marx, these characteristics of Ricardo's work rendered it both scientific and bourgeois respectively, Ricardo was the best representative of bourgeois scientific political economy. This requires some explanation.

The scientific element of Ricardo's work consists in his commitment to the labour theory of value. More or less unconsciously Ricardo retains the economic category specific to capitalist commodity production, abstract labour time as measured by value. Yet it is this very lack of consciousness on Ricardo's part that renders his theory bourgeois. For he identifies value as measured by labour time with the exchange value or price that it assumes as its form on the market. Putting it another way that we have met earlier, Ricardo grants values and prices an equal status as concepts by assuming that each exists. As a result, he cannot ask how do values become prices but only whether the two are equal or not and the manner in which they diverge.

But it would be inadequate to restrict our characterization of Ricardo's inconsistency to a discussion of his failure to distinguish value from its form. For in doing so, the discussion would be restricted to commodity production in general for which the rate of profit could be zero so that commodities would exchange at their values and Ricardo's inconsistency would not arise. In contrast, for capitalist commodity production, the rate of profit is non-zero and Ricardo's inconsistency does arise in general. Then the bourgeois element of Ricardo's theory is the simultaneous introduction of value with the more complex forms that it assumes in exchange such as wages and profits. Indeed, whilst on the kindest interpretation Ricardo might possibly have been considered to have distinguished value from price, the same cannot be said for the distinction between surplus value and profit, for the former makes no appearance in his theory and is therefore treated as identical to the latter. Just as his failure to explain the existence of surplus value and its form as profit for the capitalist economy consolidates the bourgeois element of Ricardo's theory, so his continued commitment to the labour theory of value in this context consolidates the scientific element. For whilst Ricardo's motive in retaining value theory may have been to bring the distributional relations between capital and labour to the fore, he does so with the concept of value, the economic category appropriate for an understanding of the capitalist class relations of production.

That this is so follows from the fact that value relations properly conceived lead to an understanding of the exchange relations between capital and labour as classes quite apart from the processes of exchange and therefore competition within classes to establish uniform rates of profits and wages. Rather the buying and selling of labour power at a value less than that represented by the labour time performed is the only basis for explaining the production of surplus value prior to its formation as profit in exchange.

These considerations then lead to the conclusion that the inconsistencies in Ricardo's theory are far from simple. Of particular importance is the necessary connection between the failure to distinguish surplus value from profit and the *simultaneous* introduction of *class* relations of distribution and *individual* relations of competition. Ricardo's proposition that there is an inverse relationship between the rates of profits and wages is one drawn at the level of classes for which considerations of values alone suffices. On the other hand, the attempt on this basis to establish values according to a uniform rate of profit requires that individual capitals compete towards this end. In other words, the failure to distinguish classes at the level of production, the failure to distinguish surplus value and profit, the inconsistency between value according to labour time and price according to capital advanced, and the simultaneous consideration of class relations and individual relations of competition are all part and parcel of the inconsistency within Ricardian economics.

In this light, we can examine the various ways in which schools of economic thought have resolved or reproduced the inconsistency within Ricardo's theory. Marxist theory resolves the inconsistency by drawing the distinction between the production of value (and surplus value) and its formation and distribution through exchange by the price system. As such it preserves the role played by value as a relation between classes but demonstrates how this relationship is reproduced through the individual processes associated with competition within as well as between classes.

Neo-classical theory also resolves the inconsistency, but it does so in a way that avoids rather than confronts Ricardo's problem. Faced with an inconsistency between the labour theory of value and the principle of profit according to capital advanced, neo-classical theory simply rejects any dependence upon labour time as a special contributing factor to value. Instead, it argues that differing compositions of capital are one among many influences on the formation of prices from the point of view of production, that is supply. In addition, the drawing up of supply schedules must be complemented by the conditions of demand to determine prices and these conditions depend upon the aggregated individual demands for the various commodities which in turn depend upon individual preferences or utility functions. From a Marxist viewpoint, the neo-classical theory abandons the scientific element of Ricardo's theory for a purely bourgeois standpoint. By rejecting labour time as a standard of value, it denies that category which is specific to an analysis of capitalist commodity production. By focusing on supply and demand as the determinants of price, the categories of price, wage and profit are taken for granted and remain unexplained. They are simply quantitatively determined by the conditions of supply, such as the technical relations of production, and of demand, such as individual preferences. Significantly these conditions exist in all societies so that the categories in which the specifically capitalist mode of production expresses itself are explained by those that apply throughout history. Marx reserved the term 'vulgar' for this method of theorizing because of its ahistorical preoccupation with the appearances generated by society rather than with its underlying relations. By this procedure, neo-classical economics also relieves the tension that exists in Ricardo's work because of its dual reliance upon a class theory of distribution based on value and a competitive theory of price based on the equalization of individual profit rates. It does so by abandoning any dependence upon class for its analysis, concentrating exclusively upon the economy as an aggregation of individual agents.

Apart from the Marxist and neo-classical *resolution* of Ricardo's inconsistency, there are those theories that *reproduce* it. This is most apparent in those that accept that the labour theory of value is a valuable and even necessary means of characterizing the capitalist mode of production. It yields what may be termed a 'sociology' of exploitation, revealing the significance structurally of the capitalist relations of production, the buying and selling of labour-power etc. These ideas have their ethical counterpart in the philosophy of the natural rights of labour, that producers alone deserve the fruits of their labour. But just as these morals can tell us little about the economic development of society, so the same must be said of the labour theory of value treated as a sociology of capitalism. It can only generate an approximate understanding of how capitalism develops, since it is recognized that commodities do not exchange at their values. It is as if the labour theory of value is appropriate for certain areas of analysis but inappropriate for others. Moreover, the dividing line between these areas is easily drawn. Where the relationship between classes alone is to be considered, the labour theory of value suffices. When, however, competition and the concretization of those class relations in relation to individual capitals comes to the fore, the labour theory of value must be abandoned as inadequate.

In these terms, Ricardo's problem can be seen to have been reproduced more or less directly. Consequently this treatment of value deserves the label neo-Ricardian. Interestingly, like Ricardo, neo-Ricardians argue that the determination of prices on the basis of values must be modified for a developed capitalism. However, whereas Ricardo's commitment to values based on labour time can be located in terms of an emerging capitalism and its interests in which the exchange of the products of labour becomes generalized, the neo-Ricardian commitment to value is based on an understanding of the sociology of developed capitalism for which socialist revolution is seen as the counterpart.

The neo-Ricardian label has also been applied to a different school of thought, one that we shall denote as Sraffian. It differs from the neo-Ricardian school by rejecting value theory altogether, arguing that the characterization of capitalism and its economic laws of motion is possible and indeed more satisfactorily accomplished without the encumbrance of a value theory based on labour time. In these terms, it would appear, with the rejection of value theory, that the Sraffian school resolves the inconsistencies of Ricardo's theory in much the same way as neo-classical theory. However, we will show that the inconsistency is reproduced despite the break with Ricardo's value theory.

The technical details of the economics associated with the Sraffian school need not concern us here as they have been presented in the essay on capital theory. The results developed there as a means of criticizing neo-classical theory, an assessment of the success of which is to be found in the essay mentioned, are also utilized as a means of criticizing value theory based on labour time. The Sraffians take the transformation problem as their point of departure from value theory, arguing particularly that Marx's transformation is incorrect and that correcting it would render it redundant. The reasoning runs as follows. From the technical relations of production, that is a specification of the physical and labour inputs used in the production process, equations can be derived relating prices, wages and profits. From these, the prices can be eliminated to yield an inverse relation between the rates of wages and profits. If either of these is known, so is the other and prices can then also be calculated. Consequently once the level of wages is known in real terms, the technical conditions of production suffice to determine prices. Moreover, it can be shown that knowledge of values alone, that is of the different c, v and s for each sector, is insufficient to determine either prices or the rate of profit. This follows from the fact that value inputs as well as the single output concerned have to be transformed into prices. Although we know the aggregate value of the constant capital used, we cannot transform it without knowledge of the individual means of production of which it is composed, because each different value input requires a different transformation factor. The extra information necessary to accomplish the desired transformation is nothing short of the technical conditions of production themselves. But these already suffice to determine the price relations without any reference to values whatsoever. It follows that values are an irrelevant detour in the derivation of prices.

This reasoning has been summarized in diagram 6.1. The arrows from A to B and from A to C represent the ability to determine values and profits and prices from technical and wage data. The broken line from B to C represents the impossibility of determining profits and prices from knowledge of value quantities. So much for the formal arguments of the Sraffian school. But what is its relation to Ricardian economics? As we have seen in another essay on capital theory, the Sraffian school has certain affinities with neo-classical economics. Both schools begin with given production possibilities with the object of deriving price, wage and profit equations from the conditions of individual profit maximization and perfect competition. Both also share a form of axiomatic logic. From a set of assumptions, such as those just given, other propositions are deduced, concerning for example the inverse relation between wages and profits. This process of deduction is then confused with the process of determination or causation. To give a simple example of the error caused by such confusion, suppose I do not have a head-

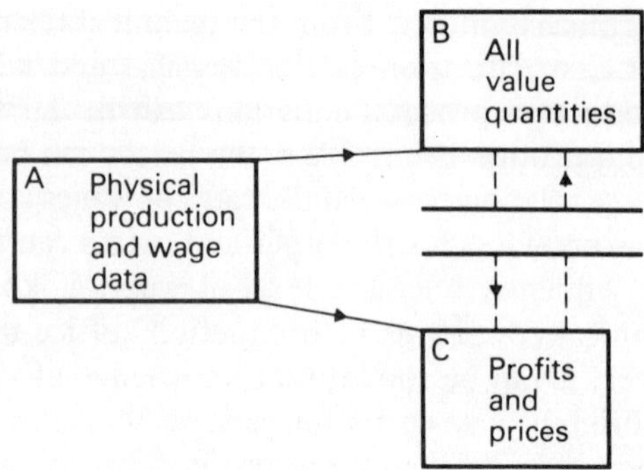

Diagram 6.1

ache because I took an aspirin. The one proposition implies the other. But it cannot be argued that the lack of headache determined or caused the taking of aspirin! By the same token, because values may not be necessary in the mathematical derivation of prices and profits, this by no means implies that values are irrelevant in explaining or determining them.

Despite sharing these characteristics with neo-classical economics, Sraffian economics also has elements in common with Ricardian economics. First, it does not distinguish value from its form, simply calculating values from technical conditions of production without relating these calculations to the social significance of the way in which value exists. Second, like neo-Ricardian economics and explaining the identification of it with that school, it argues that there is an inverse relation between wages and profits. Where it differs from Ricardian and neo-Ricardian economics is in its expressing this result in terms of physical goods as opposed to values. This is hardly surprising since Sraffians assert that values are an irrelevant detour for political economy; they are hardly going to retain them in their own analysis. The replacement of values by physical goods is particularly exemplified by the construction of the standard commodity as proposed by Sraffa. Ricardo's problem of finding an invariable standard of value is solved by determining that physical bundle of goods which, if used as *numeraire* (thereby side-stepping the problem of the money commodity), will lead to increased prices for wage decreases for those goods with higher composition of capital and the opposite for those with lower.

Quite clearly then Sraffians occupy something of a half-way house between neo-Ricardian and neo-classical economics. But where does this lead them in relation to Ricardo's inconsistency? According to their own arguments, they have eliminated the inconsistency by discarding values. Indeed they pride themselves on the consistency of the axiomatic method of deduction. However, let us discover whether Sraffians have eliminated the inconsistency in Ricardo by an oblique approach to this question. Let us consider their relation not to Ricardian but to neo-classical economics. We have already observed that there are many similarities between the two schools: exogenously given technical conditions of production, individual profit maximization on the part of capitalists, perfect competition, and associated with the failure to distinguish value from its form, the failure to explain the existence of prices, wages and profits by taking them for granted. It is more difficult to find a difference between the two schools than it is to find points of agreement! This should not come as a surprise, for as we have argued in the essay on capital theory, Sraffian economics reconstructs the price equations associated with production or supply for a neo-classical economics that is generalized from one to a many good economy. Where Sraffians diverge from neo-classical economics is in their rejection of its demand theory based on utility maximization. For neo-classical economics, the inverse relations between the rates of profits and wages is to be supplemented by one determined by the aggregation of the effects of individual preferences for future as opposed to present consumption (the rate of profit/interest representing the discount factor available to all individuals) and for leisure as opposed to the disutility of work (the price of one relative to the other being the real wage). Instead, Sraffians determine the rates of wages and profits by reference to the class struggle between capital and labour over distribution a struggle which significantly is introduced like the neo-classical utility theory completely from outside the already established reasoning behind the wage-profit relationship.

It is in this manner, in diverging from neo-classical economics, that Sraffians reintroduce, that is reproduce, Ricardo's inconsistency. However, they do it not at the level of values, for these have been exorcized, but in their considerations of physical products. They do it by their inconsistent reliance upon an analysis based at one point on aggregated individual behaviour and at another point on the relationship between classes. The first point occurs in the construction of the price equations for which the economy is simply an aggregate of individual economic agents in competition. The fact that equal rates of profits and wages are paid to capitalists and workers should not blind us to the fact that the analysis concerns individuals not classes. Indeed, the Sraffian model would be made more 'realistic' by assuming segmented markets for capitalists and labourers depending upon differences in skills, mobility and competition. It is more realistic, the more it is broken down into individual economic units that replace any reference to class. Yet, completely counterposed to this analysis is one that asserts the economy is divided into two classes whose struggles over distribution determine the rates of wages and profits. For consistency, the theory cannot contain both modes of reasoning simultaneously.

Nor is this resulting inconsistency simply arbitrary. It concerns the class relations of capitalist production indirectly, by focusing upon uniform rates of wages and profits, these being the categories of distribution specific to capitalism. But these distributional categories are individualized and rendered without class content when located in an analysis governed by individual optimizations (capitalists maximize profits) coordinated by competition through exchange. This is precisely the terms in which the Ricardian inconsistency is to be characterized, only for Sraffian economics we find it veiled by its presentation in terms of physical quantities rather than values.

It is necessary to conclude this essay by observing that an analysis based on class is not necessarily inconsistent with one that includes consideration of individual economic agents. It is necessarily so for an analysis based on axiomatic deductions, as in Sraffian economics, since one axiom basing deduction on individual economic agents is inconsistent with another based on classes unless the latter is simply the aggregate of the former. If the aggregate behaviour does differ, as for example in the transformation problem where commodities exchanging at values is replaced by commodities exchanging at prices, then the class analysis is usually considered a first approximation by the axiomatic method of theorizing. By their very nature, approximations demand to be improved upon, and the improvement, which is here equivalent to individualization, necessarily renders the first approximation invalid by the second, the second by the third and so on as the analysis becomes more 'realistic'. Here we have written in general terms, how Ricardian economics becomes Sraffian and Sraffian economics becomes neo-classical – the scientific element of Ricardo becomes replaced by the vulgar preoccupation with appearances of the realism of higher order approximations.

Marxism, however, is not based upon the axiomatic method, although this does not mean that it contains inconsistencies from the point of view of axiomatic deduction. Like all theories it can do so, if in error, one case being Marx's treatment of the transformation problem. These errors can be corrected for Marxism, they cannot for Ricardo, neo-Ricardians and Sraffians for these depend upon an inconsistency in one form or another for their very theoretical existence. How then does Marxism cope with movement of analysis at the level of classes to consideration of competition within classes and the action of individual economic agents? The answer is to be found in the Marxist method of abstraction. In contrast to the use of successive approximations by the axiomatic method of deduction, this method does not reject the simpler abstract categories, such as class, as the analysis becomes more complex. Rather it demonstrates how, for example, the underlying class relations are reproduced and how they are connected to the more complex relations of distribution, competition and exchange. In this essay, we have shown how this applies to values, their connection to capitalist class relations, and their reproduction and formation through exchange as prices. Here we see that the Marxist distinction between value and its form, which has been an important theme throughout this essay, represents more than a simple conceptual break with Ricardian definitions of value based on labour time. It goes to the very heart of the method to be employed in political economy, rejecting the process of successive approximation that increasingly focuses on vulgar appearances alone. At the same time, the concept of causation associated with axiomatic deduction is displaced by a construction of causation on the basis of the relationships that emerge between the categories of the analysis. For example, the dependence of prices upon values is found in association with the exposition of the economic structure of the capitalist mode of production, its class relations, its dependence upon the production of commodities embodying surplus value, etc. It does not construct causation on the ahistorical and universal basis associated with axiomatic deduction. These profound differences in the method and content of the various analyses may appear to have little significance in the static formulation of the transformation problem. But much can follow from small beginnings when the laws of capitalist accumulation are to be understood.

Further Reading

For a history of the labour theory of value see R. Meek, *Studies in the Labour Theory of Value,* Lawrence and Wishart, 1956. A debate on the Sraffian interpretation of the labour theory of value is to be found in the *Socialist Register,* 1977, eds., R. Miliband and J. Saville, Merlin Press.

See also I. Steedman, *Marx after Sraffa,* New Left Books, 1977; B. Fine and L. Harris, *Rereading Capital,* Macmillan, 1979, chapter 2; S. Himmelweit and S. Mohun, 'The Anomalies of Capital,' *Capital and Class,* 6, 1978; I. Gerstein, 'Production, Circulation and Value: The Significance of the "Transformation Problem" in Marx's Critique of Political Economy,' *Economy and Society,* vol. 3, 1976, and A.K. Sen, 'On the Labour Theory of Value: Some Methodological Issues,' *Cambridge Journal of Economics,* Maurice Dobb Issue, 2.2, 1978

7

Towards a Critical Dissection of Economic Theory

i. The Origin of the Elements of Economic Theory

For bourgeois economics, the history of economic thought constitutes an evolution from the doctrines of the past to the science of the present. Theories are assessed in terms of the extent to which they correspond, possibly in embryonic form, to the existing principles. Where this correspondence is absent, the elements concerned are dismissed as a source and an evidence of confusion, irrelevance or inconsistency. How well does Adam Smith's theory of laissez-faire correspond to general equilibrium theory? Ricardo's theory of differential rent is to be seen as the foretaste of marginal productivity theory. The problem of classical political economy is its neglect of demand considerations both in aggregate because of adherence to Say's Law and between goods because of the absence of utility theory. So run the traditional discussions.

In contrast, we have argued in Chapter 1, that economic theory including its modern versions should be assessed according to different principles. First, it tends to focus on an uncritical analysis of appearance, the forms in which capitalist relations present themselves. Second, bourgeois economics has the function of contributing to the ideology of the ruling class, thereby supporting and promoting the material relations of exploitation. Finally, economics has the function of providing the science by which economic policy can be formulated thereby resolving conflicts both within and between classes without threatening the social order of capitalism. What these insights leave unexplained, however, is why economics takes the specific forms that it does. Why is there a focus on one set of appearances rather than another, for example, and why are those appearances analysed in the way that they are? How is the economics formed to correspond to the strategic or ideological needs of the underlying society?

Before attempting to answer these questions, recall that theory like ideology is neither simple nor necessarily consistent and coherent. It is often drawn from a number of conflicting principles. For example, in Chapter 6, we saw that Ricardo's value theory contains inconsistency, and that his inconsistency is reproduced in many theories and in many ways. Similarly, Adam Smith utilises different notions of what constitutes a capitalist, as independent labourer at one time, as employer of labour at another. Perhaps it can be argued that these uses are sequential in the development of Smith's thought so that they do not lie side by side and create an inconsistency. Yet Smith's value theory in the *Wealth of Nations* is threefold. The labour theory of value, based on labour embodied as for Ricardo, is drawn from the rude society composed of deer and beaver hunters, a society in which commodity production would not even be necessary since hunting can be undertaken according to personal demand. The components theory, whereby the price of each commodity is reduced to the three parts comprising wages, profits and rents, clearly has its origins in a fully developed capitalist economy. Finally, Smith's treatment of labour commanded as a measure of value can be seen to be influenced by physiocracy, the economics of feudalism. The labour commanded by a commodity represents the quantity of labour it will set in employment through exchange. Physiocracy concerned itself with the *agricultural* surplus as a means of employing, that is of commanding, non-agricultural labour. Smith applies this physiocratic notion to a *general* surplus to measure the labour that can be commanded by capital.

Whilst Smith may not employ inconsistent concepts of what constitutes a capitalist simultaneously, he certainly does so employ his concepts of value and its measure. Indeed, Ricardo decisively criticises Smith for those inconsistencies that are inconsistent with his own theory; Ricardo accepts labour embodied but rejects the components theory and labour commanded. In doing so, as we have seen, Ricardo creates his own inconsistencies. Unlike Smith's that are based on the simultaneous employment of categories drawn from the rude, feudal and capitalist organizations of society, Ricardo's inconsistency is based upon the simultaneous employment of categories drawn from two different stages of capitalist development, one at which commodities do exchange at their values and one when they do not. What concerns us here is not so much that these inconsistencies exist but the nature of their origins. For

Smith, as for Ricardo, the theory and its inconsistencies are produced by the simultaneous use of understandings drawn from different modes of production or different stages of development of a mode of production. Nor is this a characteristic peculiar to classical political economy. Neo-classical economics, for example, utilises a well-recognized and often criticized atomization of the economy into individual agents. It has the effect of treating the economy as if it were simply a system of independent commodity producers. Consequently, as I have shown elsewhere (Fine (1977)) the theory finds it impossible to yield a consistent explanation of the category of profit without a degeneration into reliance upon an explanation based on the ahistorical interaction of abstinence and the productivity of time. In other words, neo-classical economics attempts to build its explanations upon categories that apply to all modes of production rather than drawing upon an explanation constructed on the basis of one or two.

What we are suggesting is that economic theory is constructed on the basis of one or more modes of production by questions like — what would capitalism be like if it were feudalism or the rude society (as for Adam Smith), or what would capitalism be like if it were at a stage where commodities exchange at their values (as for David Ricardo), or what would capitalism be like if it were simple commodity production or the same as any other economy (as for neo-classical economics)? The result is invariably some sort of inconsistency because capitalism is not feudalism, for example, and so can neither be explained nor consistently analysed by the imposition of feudalism upon it. The surplus for feudalism takes the form of rent, for capitalism the form of profit (although not exclusively), so that a theory of capitalism as feudalism will confuse capitalist profit with feudal rent and find itself in difficulty when attempting to explain rent under capitalism. Despite these inconsistencies, the resulting theories are not necessarily worthless. For an understanding of capitalism drawn from a non-capitalist mode of production is perhaps more likely to shed critical light upon capitalism than an understanding drawn from the superficial appearances of capitalism itself. Here we have the clear example of Ricardo's economics. His labour theory of value, which can only consistently be applied to a capitalism at a stage of development where commodities exchange at value, unconsciously appropriates the category specifically necessary for a critical analysis of capitalism at higher stages of development.

To dissect an economic theory, it is necessary then to identify the modes of production and the stages of their development that the theory relies upon in constructing its concepts. What we have seen is that in general an economic theory does not draw exclusively upon the mode of production and its stage of development in which it is situated. Nor, indeed, does it necessarily rely exclusively upon appearances drawn from its immediate historical vicinity. Although there are liable to be present elements corresponding to an emerging or declining economic order, other elements may be present. Smith, for example, borrows from capitalist, feudal and rude societies, neo-classical economics from all societies. It follows that whilst economic theory does develop in response to movements in the economy itself, it does not do so by substituting an analysis of the emerging appearances for those of the immediate past. Economic theory will have a more complex relation to the prevailing economy, drawing upon understandings corresponding to many forms of economic organization. Which forms of economic organization will constitute the elements that are combined to produce the theory cannot be pre-determined. It will depend upon the practice in which the economic theory is employed. It is to the illustration of these principles that we now turn by making a brief excursion into the history of economic thought.

ii. From Classical Political Economy to Marginalism

The significance of classical political economy for the development of the bourgeois economy is its formulation of a theory in which the antagonism between capital and landed property can be accommodated. With Ricardo it reaches both its fullest development, but also its limits. Theoretically, the Ricardian system is caught between stages of capitalism for which commodities exchanging at values become commodities exchanging at prices of production. By utilizing labour time as the source of value, Ricardo develops a theory of differential rent in which value for agriculture is determined by the labour-time of production on the worst land in use (or more exactly the last unit or dose of capital in use). The worst land pays no rent, but the better lands appropriate the surplus product relative to the worst land in use. With the movement onto worse land as accumulation proceeds, rents rise and profitability falls as the value of corn wages increases. The resulting movement towards and ultimately around a stationary state, for which the last land in use barely provides normal profit and subsistence wages, can only be postponed by exporting the margin of cultivation abroad, by importing corn. The existence of a tariff on corn raises rents and hastens the arrival of the stationary state. Consequently, free trade is the policy advocated by Ricardo. It is a policy further supported by his theory of comparative advantage, for which each country should specialize in the production of the commodity in which it has an advantage *relative* to the others, even if it is *absolutely* less productive in the manufacture of all commodities. For many, Ricardo's theory of comparative advantage is the perfection and generalization of Smith's theory of absolute advantage. Smith suggests that each commodity should specialize in the production of commodities in which it is absolutely more productive than others. It does not appear to occur to him that this may leave certain countries without any production at all. Smith's theory of international trade then is drawn by an analogy with trade within a country, where competition would ultimately ensure the establishment of absolute advantage. In contrast, Ricardo has a clear recognition of the existence of trade between countries at absolutely different levels of development. The substitution of comparative for absolute advantage is not simply a generalization of theory, but a recognition of the conditions for free-trade imperialism.

With the Repeal of the Corn Laws, the need to produce a theory of rent that distinguishes between land and capital vanishes. Each may be considered as a factor of production, even if land is seen in some sense as non-reproducible. With labour in addition, the three great classes of classical political economy become the three factors of production, with the peculiarity that each has a special name for its form of revenue, wage, rent and profit. In the transition between classical political economy and marginalism, the identification of land with capital as factors of production, of rent with profit, so that neither is explained, is necessarily made explicit. The theory of differential rent for agriculture must be generalized to apply to industry as a whole. Even Ricardo makes this observation, although pursued to its logical conclusions, the already shaky foundations of his value theory would be destroyed. In the space between classical political economy and marginalism, elements are drawn from both theories, focusing around the question of what makes for differential surplus (i.e. rent) in agriculture makes for differential surplus (i.e. profit) in industry for capital.

For J.S. Mill, who confesses himself a Ricardian, the case is made most explicitly.

> Extra profits analogous to rent are more frequent in the transactions of industry than is sometimes supposed ... wages and profits represent the universal elements in production, while rent may be taken to represent the differential and peculiar: any difference in favour of certain producers, or in favour of production in certain circumstances, being the source of a gain, which, though not called rent unless paid periodically by one person to another, is governed by laws entirely the same with it. The price paid for a differential advantage in producing a commodity cannot enter into the general cost of production of the commodity. (*Principles,* Book III, ch.v.para 4)

What we have here is not only the treatment of differential profit as rent but also the beginnings of an enquiry into the causes of those circumstances that create differential profit and an explanation of the level of prices by the margin in industry.

If Mill may be said to have one foot in the camp of classical political economy and one raised above the fence dividing it from marginalism, W.S. Jevons can be seen to have completed the leap. In *The Coal Question,* written in 1863, he demonstrates a remarkable genius for accommodating the propositions of classical political economy with an emerging marginalism. For Jevons, the Repeal of the Corn Laws shifts the extensive margin for corn abroad, but in the domestic economy it is passed onto the coal-fields which are the basis for producing British exports to pay for imports. Just as for Ricardian agriculture, the extensive margin for mining coal becomes more costly. Under the Malthusian pressure of geometric population growth and at the best, arithmetic growth of output, the economy is propelled towards a stationary state. Significantly, then, the margin of scarcity has been shifted (to coal), although the limits to expansion remain located in the natural conditions of the land. By the time, the *Principles of Political Economy* is published in 1871, Jevons has generalized his considerations of scarcity to the relative use of factors of production and final goods in production and consumption, respectively. In doing so, the margin of Ricardian rent theory is itself generalized to include all industry together with considerations of the relative scarcity of goods in production and consumption. With the consolidation of marginalism in Marshall's *Principles of Economics,* the revolution in economic thought is complete. But even there, the contradictory origins of marginalism, in the Ricardian theory of rent applied to industry, make an explicit appearance. Marshall notes that investment already made, fixed capital for example, is for marginalism a fixed factor of production akin to land. It will earn a return determined by its scarcity and use, and not one necessarily related to its historic price or present cost of reproduction. In other words, it bears a return analogous to rent, rather than a rate of profit, but because it is a return paid to capital and not to land Marshall utilizes the term 'quasi-rent.'

We have discussed the passage from classical political economy to marginalism without making explicit the stimulus from the economy that produces the marginalist school. In the second half of the nineteenth century, the capitalist economies were accelerating into the machine age. Increasingly, machinery was being used to displace labour from the process of production as a means by which productivity and profitability could be increased. These increases had to be set against their additional cost, or more exactly, the associated costs of production relative to other methods of production. The point is that revolutions in the methods of production are to be associated with differential profitability, only, in this case, these differences are not determined by the differences in fertility or location for the same methods of production as in the Ricardian theory of agricultural rent. They are determined by the method of production chosen. In addition, then, the theory of choice between different methods of production becomes necessary, a choice between a higher or lower capital intensity, more or less capital relative to labour according to relative prices. The result is that marginalism as such is not the fundamental feature of the marginalist revolution, although it is essential to it. As neo-classical economists looking back on Ricardo have observed, his extensive (and intensive) margin might just as well have been analysed in terms of the use of infinitesimal increments in capital as the lumps of capital or doses as it came to be called. What is fundamental to the marginalist revolution, and what frees it from any influence from classical political economy, is the generalization of differential rent/profit to the economy as a whole and the analysis of these differentials by reference to differences in techniques of production, capital-labour ratios. For this, the margin is essential so that margins can be compared as the basis for choice between capital and labour. If there were only one margin, as in Ricardian rent theory (for which the intensive margin is comparable to an application of capital to new land rather than a choice between factors of production), the problem of choice between margins cannot arise. To sum up the marginalist revolution is constituted on the principle of *substitution* rather than on the margin as such. The margin is the means by which that substitution is theorized.

We have already argued that neo-classical economics treats capitalism as if it were a system of independent commodity producers. It is paradoxical for it to do so because it seeks to explain the levels of wages and profits, direct reminders that there are workers and capitalists, and one is employed by the other. That it can do so is due to its treatment of consumption by analogy with production. Each individual's utility function represents the technology by which pleasure and pain are produced in response to the goods consumed or work done. Each worker then is a producer of utility as well as a producer of goods, only the utility is produced indirectly through the sale and performance of labour. The worker and capitalist meet as independent and free economic agents in the market place, and the same is true of the exchanges between capitalists. The result is the creation of an efficient and harmonious equilibrium in which the realm of freedom is expanded. This is not, however, simply a product of the logic of the theory. The precondition for capital to move into its machine-age and associated large-scale production is that a freely mobile labour force be available, unrestricted by the labour legislation of pre- and underdeveloped capitalist relations. The worker more or less gains the choice of an employer, but not the freedom from wage-slavery. For the capitalist too the realm of freedom is apparently expanded. The use of the credit system makes the choice between alternative methods of production a possibility, offering the maximization of profitability and the choice between present and future consumption according to the amount to be saved/invested. What is in reality the coercive force of competitive accumulation which makes itself felt through exchange relations, is thereby rendered by marginalism into an expansion of freedom and choice.

iii. The Keynesian Revolution

The Great Depression of the thirties not only represented an intense economic crisis for capitalist society, it also led to great pressure for state economic intervention. It is the theorization of state economic intervention that has yielded the Keynesian revolution, as well as much more public economics besides. Here we focus on the nature of Keynesianism.

The massive unemployment of capital and labour in the 1930s was a direct empirical refutation of the marginalist illusion that the market could achieve an efficient, full-employment equilibrium. Even the doctrine that wages were too high could only explain unemployment of labour, not of capital. For Keynes, bred in the marginalist tradition, it is not surprising that he rejected the marginalist model within its own terms of reference, the imperfect rather than perfect working of the market and exchange system. The problem of ineffective demand and the rejection of Say's Law were not, however, Keynes's innovations. He himself praised Malthus on the question and regretted that economic theory had not evolved from Malthus's insights. Malthus had argued that landlords played a crucial role by spending rent as revenue, and that by reducing their revenue, through taxes for example, the employment provided by their expenditure would be lost. The argument of Ricardo, adhering to Say's Law, is that the expenditure is not lost since it exists in the form of tax revenue, the presumption being that any income will be spent. What is significant in Malthus's argument is that it is drawn from considerations of the feudal economy. The problem considered is the expenditure of the agricultural surplus upon non-agricultural goods and services.

In this light Keynes has the same relation to Malthus as classical political economy has to physiocracy. Whereas classical political economy generalizes the concept of labour as a source of value from agriculture to industry as a whole, Keynes generalizes the problem of the *expenditure* of the surplus from agriculture to the economy as a whole. In the simple multiplier model, the question is formulated in terms of excessive saving, the equilibrium level of employment is inversely related to the saving rate. As economies become more wealthy, the saving rate increases as a psychological propensity. This is a way of saying that the surplus is proportionately increasing, and defective demand is the result of this surplus being saved rather than consumed. Just as Malthus needs the landlords to consume the surplus so Keynes needs a high propensity to consume within the economy as a whole. The parallels between Malthus and the Keynesian system are, however, more clearly presented in the formulation originating with Kalecki in the 1930s. There national income is divided into the aggregates of profits and wages rather than consumption and investment. It is the deficient expenditure of profits that creates unemployment and the landlords of Malthus have become the capitalists of Kalecki. They may play an insufficient role in disposing of the surplus.

We have seen in Chapter 3, that Keynes's particular explanation of unemployment equilibrium depends upon his theory of the supply of and demand for money. Ultimately he makes a break with the Keynesianism that he inspired since the speculative demand for money in his system is explained in terms of the social organization of investment rather than by the aggregation of individual propensities. Consequently, his policy recommendations concern the more or less direct regulation of the overall level of investment, to set the aggregate context in which the animal spirits of the capitalist class he supported could flourish without creating unemployment. In contrast, the neo-classical Keynesian synthesis and the reappraisal of Keynes are systems of thought that are a return to the view of capitalists as an economy of independent commodity producers. The result is that the economic role of the state is essentially one of a special individual, whose interventions are to be aggregated with those of an amorphous set of other economic agents. It is for this reason that the debate between monetarism and Keynesianism is synonymous with the debate over the tendency or not to full employment equilibrium. For monetarism, the interventions of the state are an encroachment upon the attainment of efficient equilibrium, whereas for Keynesianism the state has to make the correctives that bring aggregated individual variables to a desired level. Although as a special individual the state has special powers over expenditure, taxation, money supply, etc., it cannot necessarily guarantee to make the correctives required for full employment because it does not control individual behaviour. The result is both to produce a debate over the desirable extent of the mixed economy (what powers should the state take as an economic agent?) and to justify the failure to meet economic objectives until the climate of individual decision-making has been transformed (see the discussion of expectations in Chapter 4).

iv. Concluding Remarks

We have attempted to demonstrate that economic theory has its origins in the historical development of capitalism, but that it is formulated through the combination of analyses drawn from non-capitalist modes of production and from different stages of the capitalist mode. The brief review of economic theory presented here suggests that the distribution of the surplus and its realization through exchange are open to interpretations that are ultimately intergrated with a view of capitalism as simple commodity production even if the problems of effective demand and distributional struggle are posed in terms of class relations as in neo-Ricardian and Kaleckian theory. Thus, the critique of economic theory depends upon a break from a preoccupation with the relations of distribution and exchange as such, and an exploration of the class relations of capitalist *production,* the conditions in which the surplus is produced and accumulated. A reference in the text is made to B. Fine (1977). 'The Concept and Origin of Profit', in F. Green and P. Nore, *Economics: An Anti-Text,* Macmillan.

Index